Essential Histories

The Russo-Japanese War
1904–1905

Essential Histories

The Russo-Japanese War
1904–1905

Geoffrey Jukes

OSPREY
PUBLISHING

First published in Great Britain in 2002 by Osprey Publishing,
Elms Court, Chapel Way, Botley, Oxford, OX2 9LP,
Email: info@ospreypublishing.com

ISBN 1 84176 446 9

Editor: Tom Lowres
Design: Ken Vail Graphic Design, Cambridge, UK
Cartography by The Map Studio
Index by David Worthington
Picture research by Image Select International
Origination by Grasmere Digital Imaging, Leeds, UK
Printed and bound in China by L. Rex Printing Company Ltd.

02 03 04 05 06   10 9 8 7 6 5 4 3 2 1

For a complete list of titles available from Osprey Publishing
please contact:

Osprey Direct UK, PO Box 140,
Wellingborough, Northants, NN8 2FA, UK.
Email: info@ospreydirect.co.uk

Osprey Direct USA, c/o MBI Publishing,
PO Box 1, 729 Prospect Ave,
Osceola, WI 54020, USA.
Email: info@ospreydirectusa.com

www.ospreypublishing.com

All pictures supplied by the Ann Ronan picture libary.

Contents

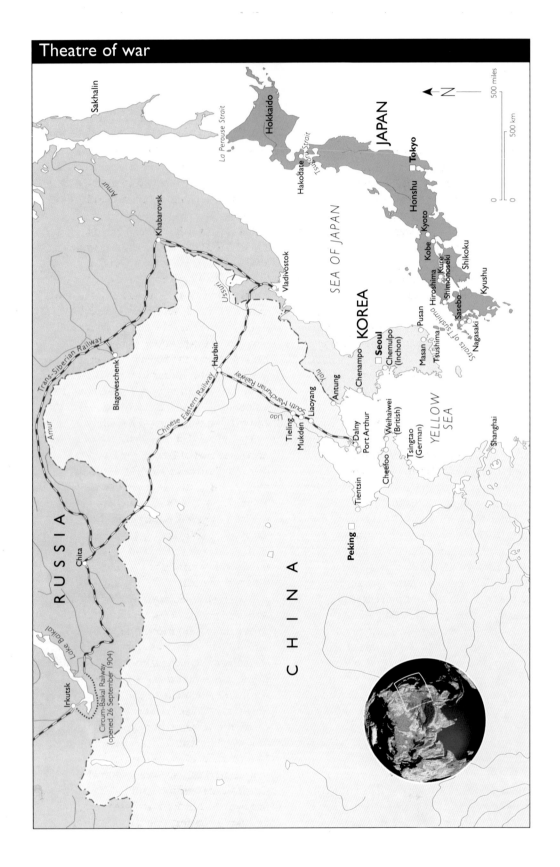

Theatre of war

Introduction

Occupying a vast plain without natural defences such as seas and mountains, Russia long equated security with expansion, protecting earlier territorial acquisitions by adding new ones. From the 1850s, prevented from expansion to the west by Germany and Austria-Hungary and to the south by the British and French shoring-up of the Ottoman Empire, the tsars turned their attention to central Asia and the Far East.

The name Vladivostok ('Rule the East'), given to the settlement established on the Sea of Japan in 1860, was an unequivocal statement of ambition, as were the treaties forced on China in respect of central Asian territories and the Amur river valley from 1860. Kamchatka had been acquired in the seventeenth century and in 1855 so had all bar the most southerly islands of the Kuriles chain, separating the Sea of Okhotsk from the Pacific Ocean. Twenty years later the Kuriles were ceded to Japan in exchange for the large island of Sakhalin.

From 1798, Alaska was Russian, and there was settlement briefly as far south as northern California. Tsar Nicholas I (1825–1856) declaimed that where the Russian flag had been raised, it should never be lowered. This did not prevent his successor, Alexander II, selling Alaska to the USA in 1867, but the sale signified not an end to expansion but the decline of the principal resource (sea-otter and seal pelts) that had brought the Russian–American Company there. Expansion at the expense of the weak central Asian Khanates continued, and acquisitive eyes turned to China's northern territory, Manchuria, and vassal state, Korea.

Russia was not uniquely expansionist. Darwin's publication of the *Origin of Species* in 1859 had an unintended spin-off, Social Darwinism, which justified subjugation of

other peoples as fulfilling nature's laws. Japan, a late entrant to the race for territory, would prove as expansionist as any, and its ambitions would soon clash with those of Russia.

For well over 200 years Japan maintained almost total isolation from the outside world, but in 1855 visits by American and Russian naval squadrons extracted visiting rights to some Japanese ports. Attempts to resist served only to demonstrate the superiority of the foreigners' military and naval technology, and in 1868 Japan embarked on a thorough programme of modernisation, encapsulated in the slogan 'Rich country. Strong army'. Individuals were sent abroad, to seek out the best 'models', and to learn the appropriate skills.

The model first chosen for the Japanese Army was that of France, but following its defeat by Prussia in 1870/71, Prussian military instructors took over in the late 1870s. The Royal Navy was chosen as the model for the nascent Japanese Navy, and naval officers, including the future Admiral Togo, were sent to England to study and train, while warships were ordered from British shipyards.

Along with this physical modernisation, universal primary education incorporating strong nationalist indoctrination was introduced. So too was a cult attached to the emperor, which claimed he was a direct descendant of the sun goddess Omikami Amaterasu, whose father, Izanagi, and grandson, Ninigi, featured in Japanese creation mythology as respectively creator of Japan and founder of its ruling dynasty. Two other belief systems existed, Buddhism and Confucianism, both 'imported' from China in the first millennium. They were not banned, but from 1889 teaching them in schools was forbidden, and Shintoism, considered indigenous, older and the 'way of the gods', was proclaimed the state ethic. It taught that those who died in wars returned to fight in spirit alongside their descendants, and that death for emperor and country was the noblest end one could meet. Buddhists could readily see that as guaranteeing reincarnation to a better life, while the Confucian emphasis on loyalty and the idea that rulers enjoyed the 'Mandate of Heaven' were consistent with Shintoist concepts of the dead guarding their descendants – and of the emperor as a living god. In this way the three belief systems reinforced each other to inspire an unusually strong national spirit.

The attention of this new Japan turned first to Korea, which had been a vassal state of China since 1644. Its location made it a potential base for an invasion of Japan, but also a bridgehead for Japanese expansion onto the Asian mainland. In 1894/95 Japan fought a victorious war against China, and in the Treaty of Shimonoseki, compelled China to abandon its overlordship of Korea and grant to Japan the Liaotung Peninsula in South Manchuria, including the naval base of Port Arthur.

Russia then acted to deprive Japan of its gains in both Korea and Manchuria. A Russian-supported coup eliminated the Japanese-backed Korean government, and Russia, supported by France and Germany, compelled Japan to return the Liaotung Peninsula to China. This was humiliating enough, but worse was to follow. The Treaty of Shimonoseki had imposed a large indemnity on China, which it could pay only by borrowing abroad. It could secure a loan only with a guarantor, and Russia undertook that role, gaining in return a number of concessions in China, including rights to lay railways and telegraph lines.

In November 1897 the kaiser forced China to grant Germany a 99-year lease of the ports of Kiao-chau and Tsingtao, and the British secured a lease on Wei-hai-Wei, to prevent

German domination of Eastern waters. This prompted Tsar Nicholas II's foreign minister to urge similar action, to counter Britain, then considered Russia's main rival. Japan was not in his sights, but Nicholas's response was to order acquisition of the Liaotung Peninsula which Russia had forced Japan to abandon less than two years previously. The Japanese government saw this as both provocative and strategically threatening, so Japan began planning for war with Russia.

Between 1897 and 1903 the Russians built the Chinese Eastern Railway, crossing Manchuria to Vladivostok and shortening the route to that port by about 350 miles compared to the Trans-Siberian Railway.

Tsar Nicholas II with officers. His father, Alexander III, had intended to teach him how to rule when he reached the age of 30, but he died when Nicholas was only 26.

The line was built to the Russian gauge, entirely Russian-administered and guarded. A new, principally Russian town, Harbin, was built to house its headquarters and as a junction with another Russian-built line, the South Manchurian Railway. This ran to the Liaotung Peninsula's commercial port of Dalny and the naval base of Port Arthur.

Russia sought to exercise economic control over Manchuria, and prevent any other country from doing so. Its General Staff made contingency plans for a war there, but did not contemplate retreats; the military topographical service therefore gave priority to mapping Manchuria south of the Chinese Eastern Railway, but a proposal in 1900 to map North Manchuria as well was not considered important enough to fund. This would put Russia at a serious disadvantage in the war, since most of the fighting was in North Manchuria. The Japanese, by contrast, employed an extensive network of spies. They were mostly Chinese, under the control of Japanese officers disguised as Chinese; and they also included disaffected, mainly non-Russian, citizens of the Russian Empire. They supplied geographical information on all of Manchuria and adjacent areas of the Russian Far East, and the Japanese were careful to pay spies far better than the Russians did, thereby acquiring a useful number of double agents.

Japanese beheading Chinese suspected of spying.

Russia's main base in north-east Asia, Vladivostok, had two disadvantages. First, it was iced-up for three to four months of the year and, second, it was on the enclosed Sea of Japan, with narrow exits that a hostile navy could easily control. The first problem was tackled by steam propulsion and the icebreaker, but the second proved insuperable. The Liaotung Peninsula ports were more attractive, not only because they were ice-free, but also because they gave easy access to the high seas. Basing warships at both Port Arthur and Vladivostok entailed dividing the Pacific Squadron, but Russia's generals did not think 'little' Japan would dare go to war.

In 1899 Great Britain launched the Boer War, and soon found it a far harder proposition than expected. By the end of 1901 it was internationally isolated, and worried that Russia would exploit its difficulties to invade India, or at least

Russians hanging Chinese suspected of spying.

challenge its leading position in trade with China. Japan stood equally alone, concerned at Russia's inroads in Manchuria and Korea and still smarting at Nicholas's actions over the Liaotung Peninsula. Japanese suspicions intensified when during the Boxer Rebellion of 1900 over 100,000 Russian troops invaded Manchuria to relieve the siege of Harbin, then comprehensively occupied all three Manchurian provinces.

Count Tadasu Hayashi, appointed in 1900 to head the Japanese legation in London, was a longstanding advocate of Japanese military expansion, and favoured an Anglo-Japanese alliance to give Japan some support against the other European powers. The British proved receptive, and a treaty of alliance was signed on 30 January 1902. It bound Britain to go to war only if any country joined Russia in initiating a war against Japan. It did not cover war initiated by Japan, but its existence reduced the likelihood of any other European

Hirobumi Ito, one of Japan's leading statesmen, strongly opposed war with Russia.

power joining Russia. Both Hayashi and Tsar Nicholas later held that without the treaty, Japan would not have dared to attack Russia.

In both Russia and Japan, leaders were divided into hawks and doves. While Hayashi was negotiating in London, Japan's leading elder statesman, former prime minister Marquis Hirobumi Ito, was in St Petersburg on his own initiative, seeking an amicable division of spoils of Korea and Manchuria. Finance minister Witte, Nicholas's most competent minister, favoured a deal, but his influence over Nicholas was waning. Foreign minister Lamsdorf refused to see Ito, and when news arrived of the Anglo-Japanese alliance, his visit lost all purpose.

With Russia's prospects of gaining a European ally against Japan reduced by the Anglo-Japanese treaty, Japan's only remaining uncertainty was the attitude of the United States. Like the Europeans, America was in

Sergey Yulevich Witte, Russia's finance minister. As minister of railways he had played a main role in the building of the Trans-Siberian Railway. He opposed Russian military occupation of Manchuria and war with Japan, but skilfully negotiated a peace settlement in 1905.

imperialist mode: it had annexed Hawaii in 1898 and taken the Philippines from Spain in 1899. This leap across the Pacific somewhat concerned Japan, but on 1 February 1902, only two days after the signing of the Anglo-Japanese treaty, the US Secretary of State Rutherford Hays, who had frequently protested against Russian encroachments in Manchuria, demanded equal treatment for all countries in trade and navigation in China. This implicitly aligned the United States with Britain and Japan, against Russia, Germany and France, dispelling Japanese fears that Russia would find any allies in the coming war. President Theodore Roosevelt was to go even further once war broke out, privately warning Germany and France that if after the war they pressured Japan as they had in 1895, the United States would side with Japan.

Chronology

1904 **4 February** Japan severs diplomatic relations with Russia.
8–9 February Surprise night attack by Japanese destroyers at Port Arthur. Japanese attack two Russian warships at Chemulpo (Inchon), Korea.
10 February Japan declares war.
12 February Japanese 12th Division lands at Chemulpo.
24 February First Japanese attempt to block Port Arthur harbour entrance.
6 March Admiral Kamimura bombards Vladivostok.
12 March General Kuropatkin, Russian Commander-in-Chief, leaves St. Petersburg.
27 March Second Japanese attempt to block Port Arthur harbour entrance.
13 April Battleship *Petropavlovsk* sunk by mine. Admiral Makarov killed. Lead units of Japanese First Army reach Yalu river.
25 April Battle of Yalu river begins.
27 April Third attempt to block Port Arthur harbour.
2 May Battle of Yalu river ends. Russians retreat.
5 May Japanese Second Army lands on Liaotung Peninsula.
16 May Japanese battleships *Hatsuse* and *Yashima* sunk by mines. Cruiser *Yoshino* sunk after collision in fog.
25/26 May Battle of Nanshan. Russians retreat; Japanese take Dalny and isolate Port Arthur.
14/15 June Battle of Te-li-Ssu (South Manchuria). Russians retreat north.
15 June Russian cruiser *Gromoboi* sinks two Japanese transports.
3 and 17 July Unsuccessful Russian attempts to retake Mo-tien Pass.

26–30 July Japanese begin close siege of Port Arthur.
31 July 'Battle of 31st July'. Superior Russian force retreats before Japanese First Army.
10 August Russian Port Arthur squadron attempts to break through to Vladivostok. Defeated in battle of the Yellow Sea. Most return to Port Arthur, the rest to internment.
14 August Battle between cruisers in Korean Straits. Russian *Rurik* sunk.
19–24 August Unsuccessful Japanese attempts to storm Port Arthur defences.
26 August Battle of Liaoyang begins.
3 September Battle of Liaoyang ends. Russians retreat north.
20/21 September Japanese capture Namako Yama and, temporarily, 203-Metre Hill at Port Arthur.
26 September Russian supply problems eased by opening of railway round Lake Baikal.
11 October Russians launch counteroffensive. Battle of Sha-Ho begins.
15 October Russian 2nd Pacific Squadron begins voyage from Baltic port of Libava.
17 October Battle of Sha-Ho ends. Russians abandon counteroffensive and retreat north.
21 October 2nd Pacific Squadron fires on Hull trawlers at Dogger Bank and sinks one.
16 November Japanese at Port Arthur reinforced by 7th Division.
26 November Unsuccessful Japanese assault on two Port Arthur forts.
30 November Japanese take 203-Metre Hill overlooking Port Arthur harbour.

6 December Japanese capture Vysokaya ('High')/Akasa Yama Hill at Port Arthur.

18–31 December Japanese take three major Port Arthur forts. Russians request surrender terms.

1905 **2 January** Port Arthur surrenders.

11/12 January Unsuccessful raid behind Japanese lines by General Mishchenko's Cossacks.

25–29 January Unsuccessful Russian counteroffensive at battle of San-de-pu/Hei-kou-tai.

19 February Preliminary skirmishes of Battle of Mukden.

23 February Main battle begins with attacks by Japanese Yalu army.

7 March Kuropatkin orders general retreat.

10 March Battle of Mukden ends with heavy losses on both sides.

17 March Kuropatkin replaced by Linevich in First Manchurian Army.

20 March US President Theodore Roosevelt offers to mediate.

28 March General Kodama returns to Tokyo to recommend ending the war.

8 April Russian 2nd Pacific Squadron passes Singapore.

21 April Japanese cabinet decides what to demand at peace negotiations.

5 May Russian 3rd Pacific Squadron passes Singapore.

9 May Final skirmishes on Manchurian front. Russians repulsed.

27/28 May Battle of Tsushima. Russian 2nd and 3rd Pacific Squadrons sunk, scuttled, captured or flee to internment in China and the Philippines.

6 June Tsar decides Russia's position at peace talks and orders reinforcements to Manchuria.

9 June US offer of mediation made public. Japan accepts on 10 June, Russia on 12 June.

8 June Japanese invade Sakhalin Island.

9 August Peace negotiations begin in Portsmouth, New Hampshire, US.

29 August Final session of peace conference.

5 September Treaty of Portsmouth signed. Japan gains South Sakhalin and Liaotung Peninsula, but no financial indemnity.

Russia's foothold in the Far East

Russia's vastness and harsh climate created problems. Tsar Alexander III had ordered the building of a railway across Siberia in 1882, but construction had not begun until 1891. Although mostly complete by 1904, a major bottleneck remained, round the south shore of Lake Baikal, where steep cliffs rising from the lake necessitated large-scale tunnel-building. Pending completion of the circum-Baikal line, two ferries were used, but their capacity was very limited, and in winter the ice was too thick for them to operate. A temporary railway was built across the ice, but this could only bear the weight of a single horse-drawn wagon. Troops had to march across the ice and entrain again on the other side, while heavy equipment such as large-calibre guns could only be transported by the ferries.

The Trans-Siberian Railway was single-track, with infrequent passing places,

General Kuropatkin was Commander-in-Chief of the Russian Manchurian Armies until he was dismissed following the battle of Mukden.

built quickly (averaging over a mile a day) and in places very shoddily. Frequent derailments and the need to go slowly to avoid more of the same further reduced its capacity. Average transit speeds over many sections were below 6 miles (10 km) an hour. This is only about twice the speed horse-drawn carts could have managed had there been a surfaced Trans-Siberian road.

Despite these constraints, the disparity in size and population of the two countries nourished Russian complacency. Tsar Nicholas believed that war with Japan would happen only if Russia (meaning himself) wanted it.

In April 1902 Russia agreed to a three-stage withdrawal of its forces from Manchuria by the end of 1903. In the summer, Russian Finance Minister Witte visited Manchuria and on his return called for its evacuation and for securing Russia's interests in the Far East exclusively by peaceful means. Only Foreign Minister Lamsdorf shared his views completely. War Minister Kuropatkin approved the first two stages, but opposed the third on the grounds that troops should stay to guard the two Russian-built railways. However, the Governor of the Liaotung Peninsula, Admiral Alexeyev, cancelled the second stage, due for completion on 8 October 1903, apparently under the influence of an adventurer, Captain Bezobrazov.

Alexeyev, Viceroy of the Russian Far East, was more aggressive than Kuropatkin and interfered in military matters of which he had poor grasp, until dismissed by the tsar.

LEFT: Marshal Iwao Oyama, Commander-in-Chief of Japanese Armies in Korea and Manchuria.

ABOVE: Emperor Meiji, though officially a god (whereas the tsar saw himself merely as god's appointee), had less power than the tsar. His duties were confined mainly to approving or rejecting propositions put forward by the government or elder statesmen.

Bezobrazov's surname (*bezobraziye* is Russian for 'disorder') was apt. A former member of the tsar's household, he had become involved in a scheme for developing timber concessions along the Yalu river border between China and Korea. On 15 May 1903 Nicholas ordered the exclusion of foreign influence from Manchuria and rapid strengthening of Russia's Far East forces. Alexeyev moved troops to a point near the Manchuria–Korea border at a time when Russia was supposed to be evacuating the entire Mukden province. Bezobrazov then succeeded in having a cabinet meeting, chaired by the tsar, endorse the creation of the Russian Far East Timber Company, with Nicholas, other royal family members and aristocrats among the shareholders. He also persuaded Nicholas to order more troops to the Far East without consulting Kuropatkin, and to put Far Eastern matters under a Far East Committee headed by his own cousin, Admiral Abaza.

News of these developments, and of Russia's refusal to implement the withdrawal agreement, galvanised the Japanese. Several meetings of officials, army and navy officers in May 1903 concluded that Russia's encroachments must be stopped. Unaware of this, in August Nicholas deprived Lamsdorf and Kuropatkin of authority over Far Eastern affairs by appointing Alexeyev Viceroy of the Far East. Kuropatkin promptly resigned as War Minister, and Witte was 'kicked upstairs'

to become chairman of the Cabinet of Ministers, a post empowered only to tell the tsar what the ministers thought. The Far East Timber Company collapsed in November, and Bezobrazov fled to Switzerland, but the damage to Russo-Japanese relations was by then beyond repair. On 23 June Emperor Meiji had agreed that, if necessary, Japan should go to war with Russia. Hirobumi Ito remained strongly opposed to war, so he too was 'promoted' to the chairmanship of the Privy Council, and preparations for war went ahead.

The military estimated that at the beginning of 1904 Japan's forces outnumbered the Russians in the Far East by 156 infantry battalions to 100, and 106 artillery batteries to 30, though in cavalry the Russians had 75 squadrons to Japan's 54. However, Russia's ability to reinforce was far greater than Japan's, so if Japan were to go to war, then the sooner the better. On 1 February 1904 Field Marshal Iwao Oyama, Chief of General Staff, appealed to Emperor Meiji for permission to go to war, and on 5 February the Emperor agreed. The mood of Japan's leaders was not optimistic, but they believed that if Russia were not stopped in Manchuria and Korea it would eventually threaten Japan's very existence. It was decided to cultivate President Roosevelt, to secure American mediation at an appropriate point in a war they were not sure they could win, could not afford to lose, and felt compelled to wage.

Relative strengths of Russia and Japan

The armies

Japan's population was then about 46.5 million. Russia's was 130 million, but only about two-thirds of this number were Slavs (Ukrainians, Byelorussians and Russians); the Muslims of central Asia and the Caucasus were not conscripted because it was thought unwise to arm or train adherents to a religion still nominally headed by a foreign potentate, the Ottoman Sultan. Russia's army had fought only two major wars since 1812, the Crimean War of 1854/56, which they had lost, and the Russo-Turkish war of 1877/78, which they had won. Its experience otherwise had been in colonial wars against weak opponents, and its conscription system provided so many grounds for exemption and opportunities for evasion that to be actually called up was widely seen as a misfortune.

The 'new model' Japanese conscript army, on the other hand, had fought well in the civil war in 1877, against China in 1894/95 and in the Boxer Rebellion of 1900. However, they had not yet faced a major power. In 1903 Kuropatkin, then Minister of War, visited Japan. He was sufficiently impressed to rate the Japanese infantry and artillery (though not the cavalry) as equal to any European army, and to advocate avoiding war. Instead he urged, as had Ito, an agreed division of spoils – Korea to Japan, northern Manchuria to Russia, and southern Manchuria to remain Chinese. Russian court and military opinion was of another mind and saw the Japanese, as one author later put it, as 'little people who lived in paper houses … and wasted hours on flower arrangement and tea ceremonies'.

Well-informed reports from the Russian Legation in Tokyo were ignored by the General Staff, which allocated only one officer (later described by Kuropatkin as a bad choice) to collate and analyse intelligence on Japan. Russia's leadership ended up knowing nothing of Japan's capability to mobilise reserves, and cherishing the illusion that one Russian soldier equalled three Japanese; ignorance and contempt were profound enough for Nicholas and many others regularly to describe the Japanese as 'monkeys', and their army as 'infantile'.

Colonel Motojiro Akashi, the Japanese military attaché in St Petersburg, relocated to Stockholm when the war began, and from there continued to control a network of agents in Russia. Their reports provided Tokyo with a very complete picture, to confirm or add to that obtained by Colonel Aoki's Far East network of numbers, locations, armaments and supply depots of Russian troops and warships in the Far East. Akashi also supported opponents of Tsarism in Russia. Finland, Ukraine and Caucasus with money, small arms and ammunition.

The navies

Russia's navy was much the larger, but was divided between the Baltic Sea, the Black Sea and the Pacific, whereas Japan's was concentrated in home waters. In mid-1902 Russia began to strengthen its Pacific Squadron, and by the end of 1903 it had seven battleships, seven cruisers, 25 destroyers and 27 smaller ships. The Japanese Navy had six battleships, ten cruisers, 40 destroyers and 40 smaller ships, and was generally superior in quality. The Russian ships were a hotchpotch of different types, armaments and speeds, and varied in the amount of armour protection they had. Their Japanese counterparts, nearly all British-built, were more uniform and faster.

A Russian epigram about postings for newly commissioned officers sent 'drinkers to the fleet, dimwits to the infantry'. Not all naval officers were drunkards, but the contrast between the shipboard living conditions of officers and those of the men were greater than in other navies, and alcohol excess was a serious problem. Baltic Fleet crews spent the six winter months ashore, because the Gulf of Finland froze, and through a bureaucratic demand for uniformity, so too did Black Sea Fleet crews, even though that sea never freezes. Ships spent little time at sea, and expended very little ammunition on gunnery training.

The Japanese Navy, under British

instructors, spent much more time at sea, and trained more intensively. Most Japanese sailors had grown up on or near the coast, and many had been fishermen, whalers or even pirates. Most Russian sailors, on the other hand, had never seen the sea until conscription. All Japanese sailors were literate, while most Russian sailors were not. The effects of that difference are unquantifiable; but steam-driven warships were the most technologically advanced weapons systems of the time; then as now, they were unlikely to reach peak efficiency in the hands of illiterates.

Scene on a gun deck of a Japanese warship during the action.

The strike on Port Arthur

Japan severed diplomatic relations with Russia on 5 February 1904. The Combined Fleet commander, Vice-Admiral Heihachiro Togo, sent 10 destroyers to attack the Russian warships in Port Arthur. On 6 February, in his flagship *Mikasa*, he led the First and Second Fleets out of Sasebo harbour – six battleships, 10 cruisers, 30 destroyers and 40 torpedo boats.

While Togo headed for Port Arthur to await the result of the destroyer attack, four Second Fleet cruisers, under Vice-Admiral Sotokichi Uryu, left to escort three merchant

Admiral Heihachiro Togo, Commander-in-Chief, Japanese Combined Fleet. His victory at Tsushima was as overwhelming as Trafalgar, and convinced Nicholas to end the war.

Togo's flagship, *Mikasa*. Shown here in dry-dock, Portsmouth, England.

ships carrying 3,000 troops of the 12th Division to land at the Korean port of Inchon (then called Chemulpo). He was joined en route by the cruiser *Asama* with 16 Combined Fleet torpedo boats, and off Chemulpo by another cruiser, *Chiyoda*, which had been keeping watch on two Russian warships, the cruiser *Varyag* and gunboat *Koreyets*, in the harbour. As the Japanese force approached the harbour on 8 February, the *Koreyets* was leaving, but on seeing them, turned back. Torpedoes from the Japanese and gunfire from the *Koreyets* were the first shots of the war; no hits were scored, and the *Koreyets* re-entered harbour. The Japanese followed, and the troops began landing. For the time being the presence of several neutral warships inhibited the Japanese from attacking the Russian ships.

The main Russian squadron was in Port Arthur. It consisted of seven battleships – *Petropavlovsk* (flagship), *Sevastopol*, *Poltava*, *Peresvyet*, *Pobeda*, *Tsesarevich* and *Retvizan*, six cruisers and one merchant ship. Conscious of the threat of war, and of the tsar's instructions that for political reasons Japan must be seen to start it, the squadron commander, Admiral Stark, had ordered two destroyers to patrol outside the harbour to provide early warning, two cruisers to sweep the entrance with their searchlights, and all ships to put out anti-torpedo nets and prepare for action. However, several ships had not yet carried out his orders, and many of their officers were partying on shore. The two destroyers, returning from patrol, found themselves in the midst of the 10 Japanese destroyers and hastened into harbour to report the enemy presence. They were still reporting when the strike came.

Just before midnight on 8 February the first Japanese torpedoes were fired. In an attack lasting only a few minutes, *Retvizan* and *Tsesarevich* and the cruiser *Pallada* were holed and sank on to the mud of the relatively shallow harbour. The Russians were too unprepared even to return fire; only the cruiser *Novik* gave chase, but the Japanese destroyers were simply too fast.

The Russian cruiser *Varyag* on its way to fight the Japanese fleet at the battle of Chemulpo where she was sunk, 9 February 1904.

Russian might and Japanese manoeuvres

Japan gains command of the sea

At Chemulpo Admiral Uryu gave *Varyag*, *Koreyets* and the Russian transport *Sungari* an ultimatum, to leave port or be sunk at anchor. The two warships attempted to break out, but in an hour's fighting *Varyag* was badly damaged and *Koreyets* set on fire. Both returned to harbour, where their captains scuttled them and burned the *Sungari*.

At Port Arthur the Russian squadron, except for the three grounded ships, was preparing to put to sea on 9 February when the Combined Fleet's 3rd Division – four cruisers under Admiral Dewa – came to investigate the results of the previous night's attack. With a good view into the harbour, two grounded ships visible, and the Russians apparently too disorganised even for their shore batteries to shell him, Dewa radioed Togo, just over the horizon, suggesting a follow-up attack by the battleships and armoured cruisers. Togo responded at once, and all three divisions in turn bombarded the town, the shore batteries and the Russian ships. The Russians returned fire, hitting four of the six battleships and one cruiser, while the Japanese scored hits on four cruisers. Again, *Novik* was the only Russian ship to attempt to encounter. It was hit once, but returned safely.

The surprise attacks before the declaration of war attracted no disapproval abroad; they were in fact widely praised in the Anglo-Saxon countries' press, which presented the war as David (Japan) versus Goliath (Russia). The harm inflicted on the Russian fleet was not crippling; one cruiser and a gunboat were lost, but the damaged ships, including the three grounded ones, could all be repaired.

The psychological effect, on the other hand, was devastating. The Japanese Navy had seized command of the sea while the Russians, apart from the *Novik*, had skulked in port. The trains from Port Arthur and Dalny to Harbin were packed with fleeing Russian civilians, and the Chinese population, barred from the trains, besieged the ships in harbour, seeking passage to anywhere. There seemed no limit to Russian misfortune (or ineptitude) at sea in the first days of the war. On 11 February the minelayer *Yenisei* and the cruiser *Boyarin* sank after hitting mines the *Yenisei* had just laid, and two destroyers were damaged when they collided.

There was, however, one success. On 24 February Togo sent five old merchant ships to be sunk in order to block the harbour mouth. The shore batteries and *Retvizan*, still on the mud but otherwise operational, destroyed all five before they were in position. The next day the Combined Fleet was involved in an inconclusive action with three Russian cruisers that came out to meet them; all three were damaged but managed to return to port. However, one of two Russian destroyers sent on a scouting mission on 26 February was caught by Japanese cruisers, and its crew scuttled it to prevent capture.

Boost to Russian morale

Russian spirits revived when Vice-Admiral Stark was replaced on 7 March by Vice-Admiral Stepan Osipovich Makarov, a hero of the 1877 war with Turkey and a prolific inventor, whose creations included the icebreaker. Just the news that he was coming brought an immediate improvement in Russian performance. *Retvizan* and *Tsesarevich* were refloated and moved to the dockyard for repair, and the Japanese noted that any Russian warships they intercepted now fought instead of running for harbour. The revival was short-lived, however, and Makarov's influence was soon removed. On 12 April the Japanese laid mines off Port Arthur and lured Makarov into bringing his squadron out to attack what he believed to be a small group of cruisers. On the morning of 13 April, seeing the Combined Fleet's battleships approaching, he ordered a return to port, but at 9.39am, with the harbour in sight, his flagship *Petropavlovsk* struck a mine and sank in minutes, taking with it Makarov and 662 crew members.

Panic struck the fleet. The speed with which the *Petropavlovsk* had sunk seemed to indicate more than the explosion of a mine. The belief that the Japanese were using the very latest of all naval weapons – torpedoes from submarines – spread like wildfire, and the Russian fleet began to fire at any piece of flotsam that remotely resembled a periscope. In fact both sides did have some submarines, but neither used them.

Half an hour later the battleship *Pobeda* also struck a mine, though it did not sink. The crestfallen squadron limped back into port, watched from a distance by Togo; then he too turned for base.

The Russian squadron's attacking spirit died with Makarov, and his successor, Vitgeft, received strict orders from Viceroy Alexeyev to take no risks. This presented Togo with a problem. Port Arthur's strong fortifications meant it could not be taken from the sea; troops would have to be landed on the Liaotung Peninsula to storm or besiege it from the landward side. To transport troops safely, the Port Arthur ships would have to be prevented from interfering; they would either have to be enticed out and destroyed or bottled up in the harbour. With Makarov gone, they were less likely to come out; so a third attempt would have to be made to block the harbour mouth.

Japan was beginning to run short of ships, but 12 old vessels loaded with stone, concrete and explosives sailed on 1 May.

ABOVE Japanese blockships fail to cut off the harbour entrance.

RIGHT Vice-Admiral Stepan Osipovich Makarov.

Three turned back when the weather became stormy, two were destroyed by Russian gunfire, and the remaining seven were blown up in positions which once again failed to cut off the entrance. Despite this, Togo falsely reported that the harbour mouth was blocked, and on the basis of his report, the 70 merchant ships conveying the Second Army left Korea on 3 May to land about 60 miles (96 km) north of Port Arthur.

Togo's gamble

Togo's willingness to risk his career and the lives of Second Army's soldiers by false reporting rested on two, or perhaps three, factors. First was his conviction that, bereft of Makarov, the Russians would not come out to challenge the strongly escorted troop convoy. Second, if they did come out, they could be dealt with by the 60 or so destroyers and torpedo boats patrolling between Port Arthur and the Elliot Islands. Third, perhaps, was the concern that if he admitted the blockships had failed yet again, the invasion would be cancelled, and his fellow admirals and the

army's generals would blame him for its cancellation and convey their displeasure to the emperor. In the event his judgement proved correct, and the invasion went ahead. Troops began landing on 5 May, with no interference from the Russian Army or Navy. That same day Viceroy Alexeyev received the tsar's permission to move to Mukden, and left Port Arthur by train. The Japanese cut the railway the next day, and thereafter Port Arthur could be supplied only by blockade-running ships.

The psychological advantage conferred by the surprise attacks at Chemulpo and Port Arthur was exploited at once by the Japanese Chief-of-Staff, Lieutenant-General Gentaro Kodama. On 16 February he landed the rest of 12th Infantry Division at Inchon, from where it was to advance to Seoul. Once the ice melted on Korea's north-west coast, two more divisions, the 22nd and the Guards, were to land and push north to the Yalu river, the boundary between Korea and Manchuria. On 25 February Korea was forced to accept the status of a Japanese 'protectorate' with face-saving but meaningless guarantees of its independence and territorial integrity.

With Japanese freedom of movement in Korea thus ensured, and with the continuing passivity of the Russian Port Arthur squadron, the 2nd and Guards Divisions were landed safely just south of Pyongyang between 14 and 21 March. They were grouped with 12th Division into the Japanese First Army, under General Tametoko Kuroki, who at once ordered a march north to the Yalu. The spring thaw made the going difficult: the roads were mostly unsurfaced; there was no mechanical transport; and there were only enough horses to pull its guns and pontoon bridge sections. All other supplies were carried in carts pulled and pushed by three men, or on the backs of Korean porters.

Japanese advance to the Yalu river

Kodama's plan required Kuroki to advance as fast as possible to the Yalu, cross it and then

attack there, to hold the Russians' attention while the Japanese Second Army landed at the neck of the Liaotung Peninsula to cut off Port Arthur by land. Kuroki's men reached the Yalu by mid-April. Units of General Mishchenko's Cossack Brigade twice attacked the Japanese advance guard, but they were easily repulsed and soon abandoned all positions south of the Yalu.

The Russian Commander-in-Chief, General Alexey Nikolayevich Kuropatkin, reached his

main Manchurian base at Liaoyang on
28 March. As former Minister of War, he knew
his forces were widely scattered and
inadequately supplied, but also that
reinforcements could be expected in the
coming summer. Having been impressed by
the Japanese Army during his 1903 visit, he
intended to avoid major engagements initially,
make orderly withdrawals and then launch
counteroffensives in late summer, when he
had gained substantial numerical superiority.

A major weakness on the Russian side was
the almost complete lack of intelligence about
the Japanese. Consequently Kuropatkin's
proposal fell foul of the ignorance of many
senior officers who, unlike him, seriously
underestimated their opponents. Among them
were Viceroy Alexeyev and General Zasulich,

Japanese troops were landed in sampans towed by
steam launches or lashed together and propelled by oars
over the stern.

Lieutenant-General Gentaro Kodama, Chief-of-Staff to Marshal Oyama and generally considered to be the mastermind behind the successful Manchurian campaign.

who commanded the eastern detachment of Kuropatkin's forces, along the north bank of the Yalu and both banks of its tributary, the Ai, opposite the town of Wiju, the centre of the Japanese line. The practice of questioning orders, disregarding or moving slowly in carrying them out would plague the Russian command; by comparison, the occasional disagreements among Japanese generals were small.

Battle of the Yalu

Kuroki was under pressure to cross the Yalu and engage the Russians as soon as possible. The river had no bridge, and Kuroki had inadequate equipment to build one, yet his engineer troops managed to remedy this using tools and forges that had been abandoned by the Russian timber firm in Wiju to make bridge sections. Preparations to attack were carried out under cover of darkness or hidden behind natural features, and patrols sent to reconnoitre the opposite bank masqueraded as local fishermen.

The Russians, on the other hand, took no steps to conceal their troops, guns or positions. The water level was low, so both rivers comprised a number of narrow, shallow channels separating sandy islands. On the night of 25/26 April the 2nd Division and Guards seized two of these islands, and the Russians also abandoned Tiger Hill, a natural feature overlooking the entire area, which provided an ideal observation point.

Perhaps the most outstanding Japanese feat of deception was in bridging. They began a construction to span the Yalu's main channel in full view of the Russians. This was a decoy, but the Russians expended much ammunition, and disclosed their artillery positions in the process, in trying to destroy the bridge. Meanwhile, out of sight, other engineer troops were using the timber company's premises and tools to build nine short portable bridges that could be rushed into position across narrower channels at the last moment before the assault.

Kuroki had been ordered to make his main attack on 30 April, to coincide with the landings on the Liaotung Peninsula. Those landings were postponed to allow Togo to first try to close Port Arthur harbour, but Kuroki's preparations were too far advanced to be altered. On the night of 29/30 April he moved 4.7in. Krupp howitzers, far heavier

General Tametoko Kuroki. Victor at the battle of Yalu river.

than the Russians' guns, onto one of the islands. On the morning of 30 May these howitzers, supported by the artillery of the Guards and 2nd Divisions, silenced the Russian guns within 30 minutes. Fighting continued until the following evening, when the Russians withdrew.

Casualties on both sides were relatively small: the three Japanese divisions lost about 300 killed and the Russians about three times that number killed or captured. However, the impact of the battle was considerable. First, it lifted the Japanese Army into the top class in the eyes of the world. Second, by showing that the war would not be a Russian walk-over, it ensured Japan could raise loans to pay for it in London and New York. Third, it put the Russians so much onto the defensive that Kuropatkin could not even contemplate detaching any troops to oppose the landings of the Japanese Second Army on the Liaotung Peninsula on 5 May. As a result, Russian land communication with Port Arthur was severed.

Japanese naval losses

For the Japanese Navy mid-May proved potentially disastrous. Between 14 and 17 May it lost a gunboat and cruiser through collisions in fog, and a destroyer, two smaller warships and, worst of all, two battleships, to mines.

Togo's main task at that time was to prevent Russian interference with the reinforcement of the Second Army, and his false report that the harbour exit was blocked gave him an additional incentive to keep the Russians in port. He therefore sent three of his six battleships, *Hatsuse*, *Yashima* and *Shikishima*, and a number of smaller warships, to patrol within sight of Port Arthur. Though he did not know it, a show of force on this scale was unnecessary, since Admiral Vitgeft had no intention of bringing his big ships out, and had had many of the ships' guns taken ashore to be installed in the forts. However, he sent out the squadron's only minelayer, the *Amur*, whose captain disobeyed Vitgeft's orders by laying

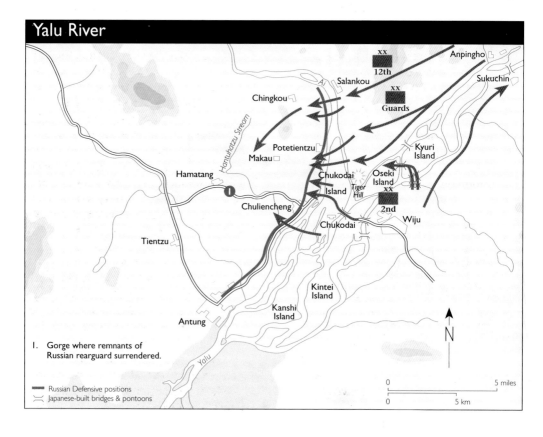

Yalu River

1. Gorge where remnants of Russian rearguard surrendered.

▬ Russian Defensive positions
⌇ Japanese-built bridges & pontoons

0   5 miles
0   5 km

mines further out to sea than usual. *Hatsuse* and *Yashima* ran on to them, and *Hatsuse* sank almost at once, in full view of the Russians on shore. *Yashima* stayed afloat for several hours and managed to get out of sight of Port Arthur before it too sank. Its loss was concealed for over a year, and some propaganda advantage was derived by persuading the generally pro-Japanese foreign press correspondents that the Russian action in laying mines in waters used by merchant shipping was reprehensible. However, the loss of the two battleships deprived Togo at one stroke of a third of his main force.

Battle of Nanshan and the isolation of Port Arthur

The Russian defences facing the Japanese Second Army at the neck of the Liaotung Peninsula were thinly held. The peninsula at this point was less than three miles wide, but the force holding it, consisting of the 5th East Siberian Regiment, an artillery battery and some smaller infantry units, faced three Japanese infantry divisions, with a fourth division and a cavalry brigade beginning arrival on 15 May. The Russians were short of artillery ammunition and had only 50 guns – a quarter of the Japanese firepower, but they had some permanent fortifications, and had laid barbed wire and minefields in front of their line. However, a rainstorm on the night of 24/25 May washed away the earth covering the mines, and just after dawn the next morning the Japanese attacked.

Their first objective was the town of Chin-Chou, north of the main Russian defence line. The Japanese 4th Division attacked it from the west, but without success, and the offensive was renewed during the night of 25/26 May, this time with three divisions – 1st and 3rd encircling Chin-Chou from the east, the 4th from the west. All the artillery was also deployed, supplemented once daylight arrived by the heavy guns of four gunboats.

The Russian commander, Colonel Tretyakov, directed the defence skilfully from a command post on Nanshan Hill, at the centre of the line, and Japanese casualties were heavy; but by midday the Russians had run out of ammunition. During the afternoon 4th Division waded through Chin-chou Bay to outflank the Russian line, and General Oku mounted a general offensive with his other two divisions to prevent any transfer of Russian troops against the outflanking movement. Tretyakov requested reinforcements, but his divisional commander, General Fok, sent him only two companies, after several hours' delay, and with instructions to use them only to cover a withdrawal.

Fok then took over command, and ordered a general retreat. Tretyakov had prepared a second line of defences, but Fok ordered them abandoned and the machine-gun and rifle ammunition dumps destroyed. His orders failed to reach Tretyakov and many of the units, so some fought on while others withdrew. The resulting confusion all worked to Japanese advantage. Only firm action by Tretyakov prevented the retreat from becoming a rout. The Russian dead totalled about 1,100; Japanese, just under 750.

The defence of Nanshan might have been more successful if Fok had used readily available reserves – at least one regiment had been encamped nearby. However, to alter the situation substantially to Russian advantage would require a great deal more. Port Arthur could resist indefinitely only if it could be supplied and reinforced, and given Japanese command of the sea, continued rail access was essential. This could only be ensured by pushing the Japanese Second Army back from where it had landed.

The defeat at Nanshan had caused the Russians to abandon the commercial port of Dalny and the outer defences of Port Arthur. However, Kodama's plan for winning the war involved a push to Russia's main Manchurian base at Liaoyang and an encirclement battle there, before Russian reinforcements could arrive from Europe; for him Port Arthur was an unwanted diversion, but the fleet there

Sinking of battleship *Hatsuse* after it hit a mine.

Battle of Nanshan

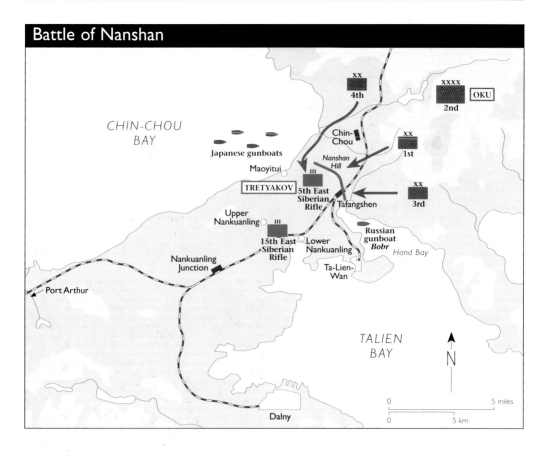

presented him with a dilemma. It had six battleships, whereas Togo now had only four. Should Russia find another Makarov, they could threaten Japanese command of the sea – which was needed in order to sustain its armies in Manchuria and Korea. If Port Arthur could be taken from the landward side, the Russian ships would be captured, scuttled by their own crews, or forced to come out and face Togo. The battles on the Yalu and at Nanshan had been won quickly; perhaps Port Arthur could also be taken quickly, in which case the advance to Liaoyang would not be greatly delayed. A further reason to underestimate the task of reducing Port Arthur was that in the Sino-Japanese War of 1894/45 it had been captured with just one regiment.

Two divisions, the 9th and 11th, designated Japanese Third Army, were allocated to the task, under General Maresuke Nogi, who had commanded the regiment that took Port Arthur in 1894. He

arrived at Dalny on 6 June, and ordered an immediate advance down the peninsula. Even after crossing the Nanshan battlefield, with its heaps of unburied corpses, and hospital tents overcrowded by thousands of Japanese wounded, Nogi and his staff remained confident that Port Arthur would be taken as easily as it had been 10 years earlier.

The command situation inside Port Arthur was confused. The governor and fortress commandant, Lieutenant-General Baron A. M. Stessel, was meant to be replaced by Lieutenant-General C. N. Smirnov, and become governor of the peninsula. However, Stessel had interpreted this as making Smirnov his subordinate, and he remained in Port Arthur, denied Smirnov essential supplies, and constantly interfered with Smirnov's arrangements for defending the fortress. The disputes between Stessel and Smirnov were known to the Japanese, who paid well for information.

LEFT General Maresuke Nogi, who took Port Arthur in the war with China in 1894 and in the Russo-Japanese War on 2 January 1905.

BELOW Lieutenant-General A M Stessel.

already in the Far East were designated the 1st Squadron of the Pacific Fleet, and ships in the Baltic nominated as the 2nd Squadron. Two days later Rear-Admiral Zinovy Petrovich Rozhestvensky was appointed to command the latter. The possibility was raised of adding some ships of the Black Sea Fleet to the 2nd Squadron, but Russian warships could not exit through the

Russia forms the 2nd Pacific Squadron

In St Petersburg Nicholas was sufficiently worried about the danger to Port Arthur to ask Kuropatkin whether he could advance to relieve it. Kuropatkin asserted that he could not, and Nicholas did not insist. He had, however, already decided to reinforce the Pacific Squadron. The decision-making process was involved, but began on 14 April, the day after the sinking of the *Petropavlovsk* and death of Makarov. On 30 April the ships

Turkish Straits without Turkey's permission, and the British encouraged the Turks to withhold it.

The core of the 2nd Squadron would be seven battleships: four new ones, *Knyaz Suvorov*, *Borodino*, *Imperator Alexander III* and *Orel*, all with a main armament of 12-in guns, the slightly older *Oslyabya*, with 10-in guns and two undergoing modernisation, *Sisoy Veliky* and *Navarin*. Secrets were hard to keep in St Petersburg, even without Colonel Akashi's spy ring, and Togo knew of its existence long before it was ready to sail. He also knew that the fleet would outnumber his four modern and one old (ex-Chinese) battleships. On 30 May he ordered 1,000 more mines laid, to keep the Port Arthur and Vladivostok harbours blocked, prevent the ships already there from moving, and stop entry by the 2nd Squadron. From then, his destroyers and torpedo boats maintained the blockade, ostentatiously laying real or dummy mines, in accordance with his orders to 'frighten the enemy'.

Vitgeft was certainly afraid, but under orders from the tsar he decided to leave harbour on 20 June and make for Vladivostok. However, he had to cancel his order after news of it was published in the local newspaper, *Novy Kray*, and he finally left port on the morning of 23 June. His six battleships (*Tsesarevich*, *Retvizan*, *Pobeda*, *Peresvyet*, *Sevastopol* and *Poltava*) led the line, followed by five cruisers and seven destroyers. After only about 20 miles, they were met in early evening by Togo's fleet of five battleships (*Mikasa*, *Asahi*, *Fuji*, *Shikishima* and the ex-Chinese *Chin Yen*), 16 cruisers and 32 destroyers/torpedo boats. Vitgeft turned back just before dark; and Togo, not wishing to risk his bigger ships in a night action, nor the possibility of running into his own minefields, sent only destroyers and torpedo boats after him. The Russian ships could not enter the harbour at low tide, so they anchored in Port Arthur roads, under the guns of the forts, to await the morning's high tide, except *Sevastopol*, which hit a mine and was forced to move to shallow water inshore. During the night the

Japanese destroyers and torpedo boats mounted a series of torpedo attacks, all unsuccessful, and the Russian guns from the ships and the forts inflicted minor damage on the Japanese ships. The Russian squadron re-entered harbour the next morning, just 24 hours after its departure.

This failure was another blow to Russian morale and Vitgeft resisted further orders by Alexeyev and the tsar to break out to Vladivostok; instead he sent most of his crews ashore to help man the forts.

In contrast to Vitgeft's passivity, the Vladivostok squadron had been very active. In mid-June three large cruisers, *Gromoboi*, *Rossiya* and *Rurik*, had headed a force that crossed the Sea of Japan, went through the Tsugaru Strait between Honshu and Hokkaido, and along the east coast of Honshu to the very mouth of Tokyo Bay. It had sunk several transports (including some carrying troops), railway engines and – most importantly – large-calibre siege guns that had been intended for use against the Port Arthur forts. Admiral Kamimura, with nine cruisers and 16 destroyers, set off in pursuit, but the Russians eluded him in fog and reached Vladivostok without loss.

Russian leaders disagree

Meanwhile at Liaoyang, Kuropatkin and Alexeyev had been at odds since the end of May. Alexeyev was insisting that Kuropatkin advance against Oku's Second Army to lift the siege of Port Arthur, while Kuropatkin was reluctant to move until reinforced. Their disagreement was referred to the tsar, who convened the ministers of war, the navy and the interior to resolve the matter. They decided in Alexeyev's favour, and Kuropatkin was instructed accordingly. Within a few days Colonel Akashi was able to inform Tokyo that an attack by the First Siberian Corps was imminent and that Lieutenant-General Baron GK Shtakelberg would be in command.

Shtakelberg proposed a staged advance, starting at Te-li-Ssu, about 130 miles from

Vice-Admiral Zinovy Petrovich Rozhestvensky, Commander-in-Chief of the Russian 2nd Pacific Squadron, destroyed at the battle of Tsushima.

Liaoyang and 80 miles from Port Arthur, and constructing defences at each stage. That the time taken to construct defences would give the Japanese time to react seems not to have entered his head; arriving at Te-li-Ssu on 13 June, he was surprised to learn that the Japanese were already approaching, and he asked Kuropatkin for reinforcements. The Russian defensive line was in small hills on both flanks and on flat ground in the centre, with a narrow valley behind, through which the South Manchurian Railway ran northwards to Harbin.

Of Oku's three divisions, the 5th was advancing along the line of the railway and the 3rd to the east of it, to assault the Russian positions frontally, while the 4th Division, separated from the other two by a range of hills, was making a wide outflanking movement around the western end of the Russian line. Shtakelberg's only precautionary measure against this had been to station a Cossack cavalry squadron with a heliograph at the town of Fu-chou, about 20 miles west of his main position. When it sighted the lead units of 4th Division on 14 June, it withdrew, but because of cloud the heliograph could not be used, and Shtakelberg was not told of the outflanking movement until late morning the next day.

Shtakelberg's plan to counterattack at the east end of the line was thwarted by confusion over orders, and it was pre-empted by Oku, whose 3rd Division overran the centre of the Russian line and shelled the Russians heavily as they withdrew. A rainstorm in the afternoon slowed the pursuit, especially 4th Division's outflanking movement, so most of First Siberian Corps escaped, less 16 guns, 477 men killed, 754 captured and 2,240 wounded. The Japanese lost 217 killed and 946 wounded. The attempt to relieve Port Arthur had collapsed before it had even begun.

By the end of June Japanese presence on the Asian mainland comprised four small armies: the First (General Kuroki), about halfway between the Yalu and Liaoyang, had three divisions (2nd, 12th and Guards); the Second (General Oku, 3rd, 4th and 5th divisions) had advanced along the South Manchurian Railway, and was only about 30 miles south-west of Liaoyang; the Third (General Nogi) was besieging Port Arthur with its original 9th and 11th divisions, plus 1st division, detached from Oku's army; and the Fourth (General Nozu) had only 10th Division, newly arrived, and was advancing north-west to join up with the Second Army, from which 5th Division would be transferred.

The supplying of these armies was a serious problem. The obvious solution would have been to use the captured sections of the South Manchurian Railway, but none of its locomotives had been taken. They could not be replaced by Japanese trains, because Japanese railways were of 3ft-6in gauge, whereas the South Manchurian Railway was built to the 5ft Russian gauge. Foreseeing this problem, Japan had had several Russian-gauge locomotives built in the United States, but the two merchant ships carrying them had been sunk by the Vladivostok squadron on 15 June. In the longer term the problem could be solved by regauging to the Japanese gauge and shipping locomotives from Japan, but in the short term it was ameliorated by building a 30-mile line from the port of Antung to Feng-huang-cheng, where General Kuroki had his headquarters. This was used to transport truckloads of supplies pushed by teams of coolies. It was built in less than two months, and was delivering its first loads by the end of June.

On the very next day Kuroki's and Nozu's divisions began advancing towards Liaoyang. The Mo-tien Pass in the mountains could have been held by a relatively small force, but Kuropatkin did not try to defend it; on 3 July he mounted a weak attempt to retake it, but that was easily repelled. Kuroki then paused to await the arrival of the other two armies, the newly appointed Commander-in-Chief, Marshal Oyama, and his Chief-of-Staff, Lieutenant-General Kodama.

On 17 July the Russians made a more determined effort to retake the Mo-tien Pass, using one division of troops from European Russia, and most of two East Siberian divisions. Although they outnumbered the Japanese 2nd Division by almost three to one, they lacked adequate gunnery support, were caught before they could entrench or disperse on the open terrain which offered no natural cover, and were cut to pieces by the Japanese artillery.

Over the next two days the 12th Division of First Army engaged the Russian 1st Division and 9th Artillery Brigade, both just arrived from Europe, commanded by General

Te-Li Ssu Fanggou

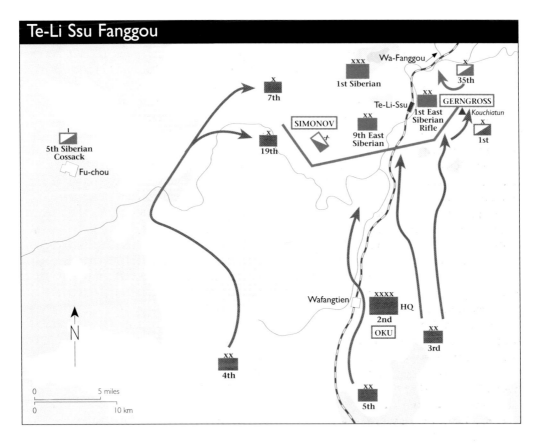

Gershelman and supported by a Trans-Baikal Cossack cavalry regiment. The Japanese plan again featured an outflanking movement coupled with frontal assaults intended mainly to pin the enemy down, and though the outflanking regiment had to make its way over hill tracks, it was attacking the Russian right flank by mid-afternoon on 19 July. The Russians again withdrew, some in panic throwing away their weapons and kit – the Japanese collected 300 rifles, 441 greatcoats and many spades and haversacks.

Oyama and Kodama arrived on 22 July and established their headquarters with Second Army. Oku attacked at Ta-shi-chiao on 24 July, again planning to combine a frontal assault with an outflanking movement. The Russians fought back fiercely until dark, but began to withdraw during the night. The Japanese did not pursue, but as the heat increased after daylight, the Russians, in thick uniforms, and hats which did not protect their necks (unlike the

Japanese equivalents), suffered many cases of heatstroke.

Kuropatkin now turned his attention to First Army, the most easterly of the three Japanese armies advancing towards Liaoyang. It was moving on widely separated roads and tracks, with mountains between them, so if a column were attacked, it would be difficult for any other to come to its support. Kuropatkin intended to attack its most easterly division, the 12th, and assembled a force to outnumber it by about two to one in infantry, with artillery slightly inferior in number (32 versus 36), but superior in range and fire power. The preparations were careful, but leisurely and obvious enough for the Japanese to get wind of them; Kuroki decided to pre-empt the attack.

Lieutenant-General Inouye, commanding 12th Division, had his men dig a line of entrenchments across the line of advance, the valley of the Shih Ho river, in front of a

Japanese field artillery.

mountain christened Makura Yama (Pillow Mountain) by the Japanese and a ridge (Shih Shan) that dominated the valley. After preliminary skirmishes on 28 and 29 July,

the Japanese attacked before dawn on 31 July, while, apart from weak infantry piquets, the Russians on Makura Yama were still asleep. The noise of firing roused them, but after several days on the mountain they had still not bothered to dig adequate entrenchments and were soon forced off. The rest of the battle was mainly an artillery duel, in which the Japanese gained the edge, despite having inferior guns. (The Japanese themselves considered four Russian field guns equal to six of theirs.)

As on other occasions, foreign observers noted the contrast between Japanese care and Russian carelessness. For example, the Japanese guns were so well concealed that the Russian artillery failed to locate most of them, whereas the Russian guns were readily detected by the cloud of dust that arose each time they fired. This fault could easily have been obviated by damping the soil with water from the nearby river. For most of the day the Russians fought well, but not without indications of low morale; prisoners said that Cossacks had been stationed behind them, with officers using their swords to prevent the men running away. This was confirmed later, when some of the Russian dead were found to have sword cuts. The Russians retreated in good order, taking their wounded with them, and the Japanese, too exhausted by the heat and exertion to pursue them, contented themselves with taking over the abandoned Russian positions.

Casualties on the Japanese side were modest – 159 killed and 830 wounded. The Russians had over 600 killed, including their commander, General Count Keller, an unknown number wounded, about 250 captured, and two guns lost. The scene was now set for a major battle at Liaoyang.

Meanwhile the Japanese Third Army, at Port Arthur, had received a large number of guns and had pushed the Russians back to their last tactical defence line in front of the permanent fortifications. Almost the whole of the city and harbour were now within range of Japanese artillery, and several Russian warships had been damaged by gunfire. The tsar again ordered Vitgeft to make for Vladivostok, and on 10 August he took the

Russian 6-in howitzer, used during the defence of Port Arthur.

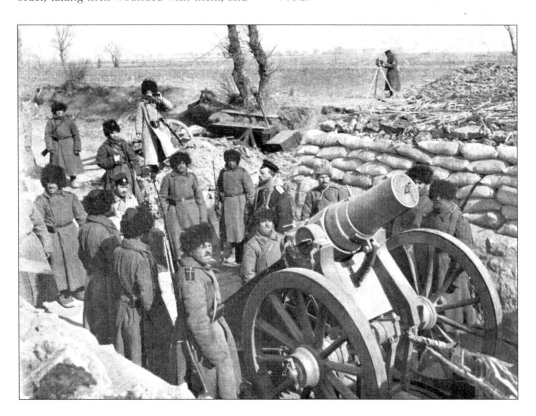

Japanese supply column using Korean porters.

squadron to sea, with six battleships, three cruisers (*Bayan* was left behind because of unrepaired mine damage) and 14 destroyers/torpedo boats. Togo was lying in wait with four battleships, 11 cruisers and 46 smaller ships; shortly before midday the two fleets sighted each other.

The battle of the Yellow Sea

For Togo, preserving his own ships was more important than destroying the enemy's, because he needed to keep his force intact against the arrival of the 2nd Squadron from Europe. After initial exchanges of fire he opted to keep his distance and rely on his light forces to attack after dark with torpedoes and mines. However, in mid-afternoon he closed in again to within about five miles and battle resumed. The Russians scored a number of hits on *Mikasa*, *Asahi* and *Shikishima*, and the Japanese hit all six of the Russian battleships, but at about 5.45pm with less than an hour of daylight left, luck deserted the Russians. A salvo of 12-in shells hit *Tsesarevich*'s bridge, blowing Vitgeft to pieces and jamming the ship's helm with the dead bodies of his staff. *Tsesarevich* swung in a circle, *Retvizan* followed, believing the flagship's turn intentional, and collisions with *Peresvyet* and *Sevastopol* were narrowly averted. The second-in-command, Prince Ukhtomski, in *Peresvyet*, decided to return to Port Arthur; he communicated his orders by flag only with difficulty, because both his ship's masts had been shot away. Togo halted his pursuit when he sighted the Russian destroyers and torpedo boats; he did not wish to risk his battleships.

Tsesarevich and three destroyers fled to the German treaty port of Kiao-chou, and were interned. Of three cruisers that ran to escape, *Diana* was interned at Saigon, *Askold*, together with one destroyer, at Shanghai, and the third, *Novik*, was the only ship to

Russian barbed-wire entanglements and foxholes.

reach Russian territory. It was intercepted by two Japanese cruisers off the southern coast of Sakhalin and after a determined fight was scuttled by its crew. A destroyer that reached the Chinese port of Chefoo was seized there by the Japanese and incorporated into the Japanese Navy.

Not knowing that the Port Arthur ships had turned back, the three heavy cruisers, *Gromoboi*, *Rossia* and *Rurik*, left Vladivostok on 13 August to assist them. Soon after dawn the next day they encountered four of Kamimura's cruisers and turned back. Kamimura gave chase; in a running fight, *Rurik* was sunk and the other two were badly damaged.

Despite only limited Russian losses – two cruisers sunk and one destroyer captured – the battle of the Yellow Sea and its aftermath delivered another important victory to the Japanese Navy. The Port Arthur squadron had been forced back to its dangerous anchorage, less one battleship, two cruisers and three destroyers interned, for the loss of

just one Japanese torpedo boat, smashed by *Retvizan*'s guns. The only Russians to reach Vladivostok were the survivors from *Novik*, on foot, after an epic 45-day march.

The captain of *Bayan*, Captain RN Viren, was promoted to Rear-Admiral to replace Vitgeft. He was no more inclined to heroics than Ukhtomski, who had fled to internment; when Alexeyev ordered him to make for Vladivostok again, Viren flatly refused, arguing that if he went out, he would be sunk, and that it was preferable to preserve the squadron for the arrival of 2nd Squadron. This argument would have been tenable had the ships in Port Arthur not been vulnerable to shelling by the 11-in Krupp siege guns the Japanese eventually brought in. Viren's mention of waiting to join the 2nd Squadron was a mere excuse: his desire to stay put was demonstrated by his removal of 284 guns from the ships to the forts.

Port Arthur under siege

The command situation in Port Arthur remained confused. Stessel continued to defy Kuropatkin's orders to leave the defence of the fortress to Smirnov, and went on issuing orders over Smirnov's head. At the same time, the tightening of the Japanese blockade was making it more difficult for ships to run in supplies for the 45,000-man garrison and the remaining civilians. On 16 August Nogi sent in a request for surrender and a rescript from the emperor offering to let women, children and other non-combatants leave. Stessel rejected both propositions, so Nogi prepared for a general assault.

The fortifications at Port Arthur were a mixed collection of coastal forts, old Chinese forts on the landward side, incomplete Russian-built redoubts and isolated battery positions joined by covered ways. An outer line of defences ran along the high ground from Louisa Bay in the west to Little Orphan hill in the east. Between February and August troops directed by Generals Smirnov and Kondratenko had built concrete walls, dug miles of trenches, tunnelled intensively into the hills, and installed many guns from the ships. They had also laid wire entanglements in front of their positions, though some of these were of ordinary wire, as barbed wire was in short supply. For all their diligence in building the defences, they had omitted to mow the fields of millet growing anything up to 10 feet high and stretching most of the way from the Japanese forward positions to their own front line. This omission enabled the Japanese to approach without being detected.

Japanese intelligence, excellent in Manchuria, was weaker at Port Arthur, and though the Japanese could see some of the Russian preparations, they did not know their full extent. Nogi seemed to be very much influenced by the ease of his victory in 1894 and believed that gunfire from Togo's ships could compensate for the loss of the heavy siege guns that had gone down in the transports sunk in mid-June. He opened his assault at daybreak on 19 August, with his 1st Division attacking 174-Metre Hill at the west end of the Russian line, a little over three miles from the harbour. It was defended by Colonel Tretyakov, who had fought at Nanshan, two East Siberian infantry regiments and two companies of sailors, holding three lines of trenches. The Japanese overran the first two lines on 20 August but the third held firm. Casualties on both sides were heavy, but General Fok, who had refused Tretyakov reinforcements at Nanshan proved no more forthcoming here. With half the defenders killed or wounded, the rest were seized by panic and many ran for their lives. Tretyakov and Kondratenko managed to restore some semblance of order, but 174-Metre Hill was lost, at a cost of about 1,100 Russians and 1,800 Japanese killed or wounded.

On the east side of the defences, 9th and 11th Divisions attacked the Waterworks Redoubt and two forts, about two miles north of the harbour. Here the Russians defended strongly against successive waves of Japanese, who advanced through trenches and ravines piled high with the corpses of the preceding waves. On the third day the sector commander, General Gorbatovski, called for reinforcements, as some of his troops began a panic flight. Fok again refused help, and Smirnov removed him from operational duties. Stessel countermanded Smirnov's order, so Fok remained.

It was not just Russian morale that was shaky; after one of the Japanese regiments had taken very heavy casualties, its survivors refused to leave their trenches when ordered to attack once more. A major who attempted to rouse them was killed by Russian gunfire; Nogi had a monument erected to the major and paraded the delinquent regiment before it daily in apology.

Another regiment began the assault with 1,800 men and four days later only 200 were still alive. All the 9th and 11th Divisions had to show for four days of fighting was two Chinese forts (East and West Pan-lung) and 16,000 casualties. On 24 August General

Nogi called off the attempts to storm the fortress, and settled for a prolonged siege.

The battle of Liaoyang

At Liaoyang, Kuropatkin was again under pressure, from Alexeyev to relieve Port Arthur and from St Petersburg to mount an offensive with the reinforcements he had received. His forces now considerably outnumbered those of Oyama (158,000 men to 128,000, 148 cavalry squadrons to 33, and 609 guns to 170). However, he was so badly served by intelligence that he believed himself outnumbered. Japanese intelligence, on the other hand, with Chinese co-operation, had very accurate information about Russian strengths and deployments.

Kuropatkin's response to the belief he was outnumbered was to prepare for a defensive battle, whereas Oyama's reaction to the certainty he was outnumbered was to decide to attack before more Russians arrived. However, Kuropatkin's decision to defend was not based solely in pessimism. The wet season, which began in July, had turned the terrain to a sea of mud, and made the two local rivers, the Tai-tzu and its tributary, the Tang, unfordable raging torrents. The weather's adverse effects on mobility could be expected on balance to favour defence over offence.

Kuropatkin deployed his forces in three lines. The outer line ran on average about 17 miles south of the walled city. Its western end, centred on An-shan-chan, covered the railway and road from Port Arthur; the eastern end, centred on An-ping, guarded the road from the Mo-tien Pass. There were light flank guards at both ends of the line, and a gap of about 12 miles in the roadless mountains between the western group (General N. P. Zarubayev) and the eastern (General A. A. Bilderling). A strong reserve group was encamped in Liaoyang itself and to the north, along the railway to Mukden.

Oyama's plan, devised by Kodama, was for the Second Army in the west to advance along the railway, while the First used the Mo-tien Pass road and tracks east of it to reach the plain, advance to the railway north of Liaoyang and cut Kuropatkin's communications. At a later stage, Fourth Army would be committed on Second Army's right. The terrain did not favour outflanking movements; frontal assaults were the only option.

First Army moved on 26 August, and after a day's fighting, forced the Russian Tenth Corps out of the Hung-sha Pass. Kuropatkin reacted to this by ordering abandonment of the entire outer defence line. Torrential rain and fog helped to conceal the withdrawal from the Japanese for several hours, but at least one artillery battery became mired in the mud, and had to be abandoned. By 29 August the Russians were back at the second defence line. This was about seven miles (11 km) from Liaoyang and ran for 25 miles from the railway south-west of the city to the Tai-tzu river to the east. Its western end comprised several small hills, dominated by a 210-metre hill, known to the Russians as Cairn Hill, where the two divisions of the 1st Siberian Rifle Corps were entrenched. From west to east the rest of the line was manned by the 3rd Siberian, 10th European and 17th Corps, a total of eight infantry divisions, with Cossack cavalry guarding each flank. The Japanese forces were, from west to east, Second and Fourth Armies, with First Army still approaching from the south-east.

Russian military mapping of Manchuria had not envisaged retreats, and had given priority to South Manchuria; this meant the Russians were now operating on almost unmapped terrain. The maps hastily produced before the battle were sketchy and inaccurate, and this would cause problems as events developed, especially as most of the ground was covered in millet fields, in which troops would easily lose their way.

The first move was made by Lieutenant-General N. Y. Ivanov's 3rd Siberian Corps, which attacked on Fourth Army's front. Oyama ordered Oku's Second Army to take Cairn Hill, to relieve the pressure on Fourth Army and prevent a Russian breakthrough.

Siege of Port Arthur

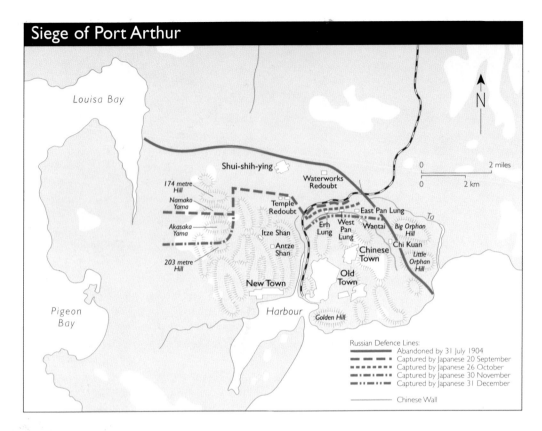

Louisa Bay

Shui-shih-ying

174 metre Hill

Waterworks Redoubt

Namako Yama

Temple Redoubt

East Pan Lung

To

Akasaka Yama

Erh Lung

West Pan Lung

Wantai

Big Orphan Hill

Itze Shan

Chi Kuan

Antze Shan

Chinese Town

Little Orphan Hill

203 metre Hill

Old Town

New Town

Pigeon Bay

Harbour

Golden Hill

N

0 ———— 2 miles

0 ———— 2 km

Russian Defence Lines:
Abandoned by 31 July 1904
Captured by Japanese 20 September
Captured by Japanese 26 October
Captured by Japanese 30 November
Captured by Japanese 31 December

Chinese Wall

Oku's troops had already been in action all day against the Russians in the small hills, and had gained no ground at all. The new attack was no more successful.

The situation was now critical for both sides, with neither realising the other had reached its limit. For the Japanese the danger was that the Russians, who had held them all day, would break through and cut off the whole of Second Army. To Kuropatkin it was clear that the 1st Siberian Corps was completely exhausted and could do no more. He still had ample reserves, but would not commit them because he still believed himself outnumbered, and was concerned at the situation on his far left flank. There the Japanese First Army had begun to move, with orders to cross the Tai-tzu river, outflank the Russian line and cut the railway. Kuroki put about half his army across, roughly eight miles east of the Russian line, on the night of 30/31 August and headed for two hills which dominated the plain and railway line beyond.

By 1 September Cairn Hill had been taken and Japanese artillery installed there was shelling Liaoyang. The increase in railway traffic seemed to mean that the Russians were retreating towards Mukden, about 40 miles (64km) north, but in fact they were merely evacuating their wounded, and Kuropatkin was preparing a counteroffensive against Kuroki's army. The latter had less than two complete divisions across the river; against them Kuropatkin planned to throw the equivalent of five divisions – the whole of 1st Siberian and 10th Corps, each of two divisions, and 13 battalions under Major-General V. N. Orlov. If this move succeeded, the Japanese would suffer a major defeat.

Unfortunately for the Russians, their communications were even worse than usual. Kuropatkin was not told that the offensive's focal point, the small hill called Manju Yama by the Japanese, was already in Japanese hands, nor that Orlov had not received his orders, and that the runner he had sent to seek instructions had lost his

Liaoyang

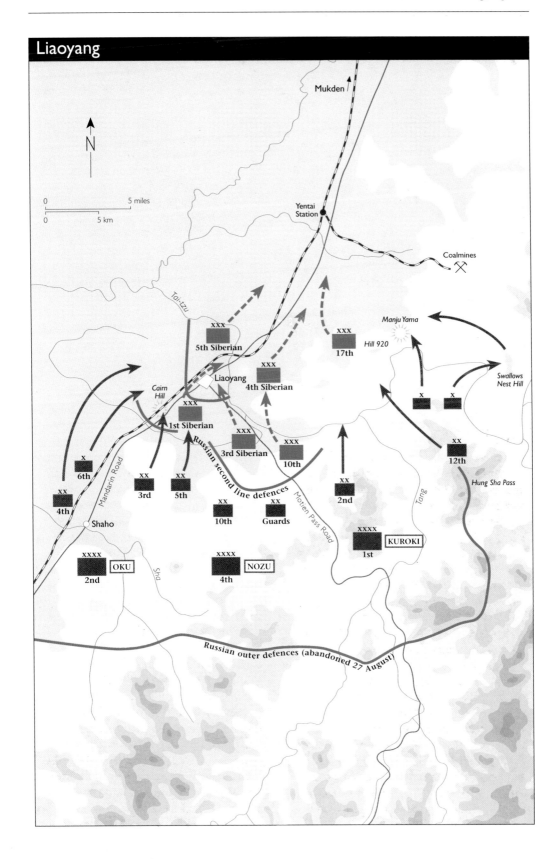

N

0 _____ 5 miles
0 _____ 5 km

Mukden

Yentai
Station

Coalmines

Tai-tzu

Manju Yama

XXX
5th Siberian

XXX
17th   Hill 920

Swallows
Nest Hill

XXX
4th Siberian

Liaoyang

Cairn
Hill

XXX
1st Siberian

X   X

Russian second line defences

XXX
3rd Siberian

XXX
10th

XX
12th

X
6th

XX
3rd

XX
5th

XX
10th

XX
Guards

XX
2nd

Hung Sha Pass

Tang

Mandarin Road

Motien Pass Road

XX
4th

Shaho

XXXX
1st   KUROKI

XXXX
2nd   OKU

XXXX
4th   NOZU

Sha

Russian outer defences (abandoned 27 August)

way in the millet. Lacking orders and artillery (also lost in the millet), Orlov decided to march through the millet towards the sound of gunfire at Manju Yama. Before long he ran into the Japanese main force, and within minutes 12 of his 13 battalions were fleeing in panic.

Shtakelberg's 1st Siberian Corps arrived on the afternoon of 2 September, already worn out by days of fighting in humid heat, torrential rain and the long march from the west end of the line. When Shtakelberg sought assistance from General Mishchenko's two brigades of Cossacks, Mishchenko claimed to have orders to go elsewhere and withdrew, leaving Shtakelberg no choice but to follow.

Kuropatkin again attempted to retake Manju Yama, and concentrated 25 battalions and 152 guns there. Fighting went on well into the night, and the Russians temporarily retook the mountain, but in the confusion, three Russian regiments fired on each other, then each fled in disorder. The troops entrenched on Manju Yama were ordered to withdraw during the night, but Kuropatkin was not told, and he ordered a renewed offensive based on the assumption that it was still in Russian hands. However, this offensive never took place, because a series of messengers appeared at his headquarters during the night of 3/4 September bearing bad news. First, Zarubayev, holding the inner defence line at Liaoyang, reported that he was running short of ammunition and reserves. Then Shtakelberg declared the 1st Siberian Corps too worn down to defend its positions. Another messenger arrived to report that the force defending Mukden against First Army's likely advance had retired to a pass only 16 miles (26 km) from the city, and finally Kuropatkin learned that the Japanese were back in control of Manju Yama, from where they could easily advance to cut the railway.

All these signs pointed to a battle lost, but most serious was the threat to Mukden. At 6.00 am Kuropatkin ordered a general withdrawal. Helped by thick mist, the Russians gained a head start of several hours over Kuroki, who did not learn of their retreat until late morning. His troops were too exhausted and short of ammunition to follow, and the torrential rain that turned the road into a swamp would have slowed a pursuit at least as much as it slowed the retreat. So the Japanese failed to interfere significantly with the Russian withdrawal, and on that basis Kuropatkin claimed a victory. In fact he had been forced into retreat by a greatly outnumbered enemy and had won only in the sense of having fewer casualties. The Japanese lost 5,537 killed and 18,603 wounded; the Russians, 3,611 killed and 14,301 wounded; but the lower Russian casualty figure owed much to panic flights or refusals to engage. It was not a good omen for future battles.

The victory at Liaoyang, though incomplete, preserved Japan's military credibility by offsetting the failure of the frontal assaults at Port Arthur. As the Liaoyang battle was ending, Nogi began digging trench systems, tunnelling under the fort walls with a view to blowing them up with explosives, and exploiting the arrival of additional guns, including six 11-in Krupp howitzers, released from Japan's coastal defences once it had become clear that Russia could not invade Japan. The arrival of 16,000 reinforcements approximately replaced those lost in the suicidal frontal assaults. Kodama paid his first visit during September, and since Nogi willingly accepted whatever advice Kodama gave, he was kept in command.

Within the fortress Stessel continued to work at cross-purposes with Smirnov, denouncing him to Kuropatkin as 'not a fighting general', sending misleading telegrams to the tsar and inflaming relations within the garrison by constant denigration of the sailors. Food was beginning to run short, horses and donkeys were being eaten, and shortages of vegetables and fruit had led to many cases of scurvy, in addition to the dysentery and typhoid cases now beginning to appear. The Japanese were also bedevilled with illness due to dietary deficiencies – beriberi, dysentery and typhoid. The beriberi

Russian field gun in millet field.

problem was ameliorated by mixing barley with the rice.

Of the four hills on the west side of the harbour, the most southerly, 203-Metre Hill, offered the best view of the warships' anchorages and positions for firing on them. Neither Stessel nor Nogi initially realised its value, but during his visit Kodama drew Nogi's attention to the importance of taking the hill. First the hill immediately north of it, called Namako Yama by the Japanese, had to be taken. Together with the Waterworks and Temple redoubts it was attacked on 18 September, and all three objectives were taken within 24 hours. On 19 September 203-Metre Hill was attacked. The higher of its two trench lines was reached during the night, but Russian reinforcements retook it and, belatedly, began fortifying the position.

Nogi now had over 400 guns, and the harbour and town were under regular fire. The damage done to the ships by shelling relieved Togo's concerns, by making them incapable of coming out to join the 2nd Squadron when it arrived. A strategically irrelevant attempt to capture the fortress as a 'present' for the emperor's birthday on 3 November led to a series of assaults in the last six days of October. They achieved little, at a cost of 4,800 casualties.

In Manchuria Kuropatkin's belief that he was outnumbered was put to rest during September by the arrival of a stream of reinforcements, including two entire corps (First Army and 6th Siberian). On 24 September the tsar decreed formation of the Second Manchurian Army, and appointed General Oskar Kasimirovich Grippenberg to its command. The new army was welcome to Kuropatkin, but its commander was not. Grippenberg was another court favourite, 66 years old and lacking in health, training and experience of command in the field beyond battalion level.

The battle of Sha Ho

Pressure to mount another offensive was now growing. Kuropatkin had claimed a victory at Liaoyang and been given the reinforcements he had sought, but the situation at Port Arthur was worsening. If it were not relieved by an offensive from Manchuria, Port Arthur would fall. Nogi's Third Army would then be free to join the three already facing him, and then he might be outnumbered again. Besides, campaigning weather was beginning to run short with winter imminent, so he should attack soon.

Kuropatkin was reluctant to venture too far, and, knowing the poor state of morale and supply, so too were most of his subordinate generals. His staff devised several possible offensive plans during September, but they were handicapped by the lack of accurate maps, and though St Petersburg responded to Kuropatkin's request for surveyors and draftsmen, Viceroy Alexeyev appropriated them for himself when they arrived at Harbin, so they never reached Kuropatkin. His staff had to improvise, producing, as before, maps that lacked contours and riddled with inaccuracies.

Battle would be joined along the Sha-Ho river, about 20 miles (32km) south of Mukden, with the Russian right flank and centre in mostly flat land stretching south to Liaoyang and the left flank in the hills. The terrain in the flat country differed from that of earlier battles only in that the millet and maize had by now been harvested, so fields of fire were improved, but cover was much reduced, mostly to villages and the clumps of trees that surrounded them.

Given the extent of the preparations and the presence of Japanese agents among the Chinese population, Kuropatkin did not expect to conceal the fact that an offensive was pending, so his proclamation of 2 October, to the effect that 'the moment for the attack so ardently desired by the army' had arrived, and that 'the moment has come for us to impose our will on the Japanese' told Marshal Oyama nothing he did not already know.

Believing the Japanese would expect his main attack to come on the flat land, Kuropatkin decided to confirm their expectations by advancing onto the plain on 5 October, complete with bands and banners,

and then surprise them by launching his main thrust in the mountains on his left flank. His belief was correct: when First Army's right flank came under heavy pressure on 7 October, Oyama was reluctant to accept Kuroki's assessment that this was the main Russian assault. However, he became convinced when Kuropatkin's orders to Shtakelberg to turn the Japanese right wing and, if possible, march on Liaoyang were found on the body of a Russian staff officer killed in a skirmish. At 10.00pm on 9 October Oyama ordered all three armies to advance; the next day he expanded the concept by ordering the First Army to hold its front and the Second and Fourth Armies to outflank the Russian defences on each side of the railway and road, to cut their lines of communication to Harbin and Russia.

On First Army's front Russian infantry, artillery and cavalry could be seen from vantage points in the hills, advancing in an enormous mass. Then they were seen to stop and begin digging in. As before, Shtakelberg had conceived of his advance as movement through a series of defensive positions. He complained to Kuropatkin: 'From the map, the country through which we must pass would appear to be as flat as a pancake, but in reality it is extremely hilly, and hardly passable for field artillery.' On 11 October Shtakelberg attacked 12th Division in the hills east of the Yentai coal mines. By nightfall he had 5,000 killed or wounded; 12th Division had lost a third of its strength, but the Russian offensive had stalled only a quarter of the way to its objectives. As on other occasions in the war, Russian slowness to act had given the Japanese time to retrieve a potentially disastrous situation.

The commander of the forces facing the other two Japanese Armies, General Bilderling, was required only to prevent their moving forces to counter Shtakelberg's offensive. He had specific orders to attack only after building a defensive position, then construct another before advancing further, and assume the defensive at once if the Japanese counterattacked. Once the Second and Fourth Armies began attacking,

Sha-ho

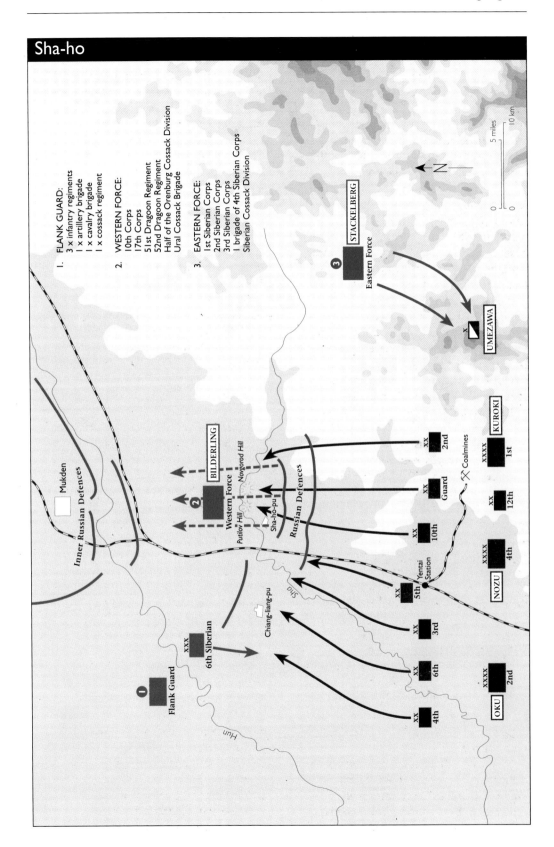

1. FLANK GUARD:
   3 x infantry regiments
   1 x artillery brigade
   1 x cavalry brigade
   1 x cossack regiment

2. WESTERN FORCE:
   10th Corps
   17th Corps
   51st Dragoon Regiment
   52nd Dragoon Regiment
   Half of the Orenburg Cossack Division
   Ural Cossack Brigade

3. EASTERN FORCE:
   1st Siberian Corps
   2nd Siberian Corps
   3rd Siberian Corps
   1 brigade of 4th Siberian Corps
   Siberian Cossack Division

on 10 October, Bilderling was pushed back, and poor Russian communications made matters worse. Kuropatkin distrusted both Bilderling and Shtakelberg, so began sending orders direct to their subordinates, without their knowledge. His distrust appears to have extended to telephones: he relied mostly on runners, which meant that an order frequently took hours to reach its destination or did not arrive at all. One order to Shtakelberg, for example, took over 11 hours to arrive.

In response to Oyama's order to advance to the Sha-Ho as fast as possible, Fourth Army took the village of Sha-ho-pu, on its south bank, just east of the railway and the main road. About two miles (3km) to the north-east was a ridge of two small hills, joined by a saddle, known to the Japanese as San-kai-seki-san (Three-Rock Hill). Though less than 100 feet high, it commanded the plain below, and so it was imperative that the Russians hold it. Kuropatkin ordered that the Japanese be expelled from Sha-ho-pu and by evening the defenders were at their last gasp. Yet once again Russian inefficiency came to their aid. The force under General Mau, meant to deliver the crowning blow, lost its way and arrived only in the middle of the night, too exhausted to be sent into action immediately.

By then 10th Division of Japanese Fourth Army had already begun a night attack on San-kai-seki-san, and by 5.00 am on 13 October it was taken. The Russians had occupied it since 9 October and had been ordered to defend it to the utmost. The Japanese commended the bravery of the defenders (the Alexander III Regiment, newly arrived from Europe), but not their failure to make any special preparations for defence, such as entrenchments, in the four days preceding the attack. This was a common criticism by Japanese and foreign observers alike. The Russians often employed Chinese labour to dig trenches or gun pits, instead of doing so themselves, whereas it was normal for the Japanese, even after a whole day's fighting, to spend the evening and sometimes the night, digging defences.

To the west of the railway and road the Japanese 4th Division (Major-General Tsukamato) tangled with the 6th Siberian Corps. The Russians' first echelon, advancing close to the railway, was soon under heavy fire and stopped to await the second echelon. On the flat ground that formation, the 2nd Brigade of 55th Rifle Division, which had not been in action before, could be seen from miles away, forming up as for parade, in close order, with banners flying, bands playing, priests carrying icons through the ranks, and the officers lining up in front of their men. When they were half a mile (800 m) away, the Japanese opened fire, and within minutes most of the Russian officers and the front ranks of men were dead or wounded. The brigade commander, Major-General Laiming, galloped to the front, reordered what was left of the force, and personally led it until he was wounded and the remnants of the brigade fell back.

Kuropatkin, who had begun the battle with six divisions in reserve, now had none left. Since fighting at the east end of the front had died down, and the Japanese First Army was itself too battered to mount a major attack in the near future, he sent a runner to Shtakelberg with an order to send 25 of his 65 battalions to him. Shtakelberg, who was reluctant to lose so much of his force, instead sought permission to use them to attack to the west. By the time his messenger returned with Kuropatkin's refusal, it was late evening; the troops could not leave until just before dawn the next day, 14 October.

The Russian offensive had so far been a fiasco, and losses were enormous. On the flat terrain of their left and centre, even an attempt to withdraw would be vulnerable to Japanese artillery on the two small hills of San-kai-seki-san, so on 16 October Kuropatkin assembled a large force to retake them. The force had three elements: the 1st Brigade of 22nd Rifle Division, to attack the eastern end (known to the Russians as One-Tree Hill); the 2nd Brigade of 5th East Siberian Rifle Division to attack the western end; and the 36th East Siberian Rifle Regiment to provide flank and rear support. Like the previous Japanese attack, the recapture was to be a night operation, on 16/17 October. Unlike the Japanese assault, however, there was no element of surprise. The Japanese on the ridge had an excellent view of the force assembling before dark on 16 October, and duly reported to Oyama. He and Kodama thought it much too large a force for such a limited objective and concluded it was meant for a major assault against Second Army along the railway and road. Oyama therefore refused requests for reinforcement of the ridge by the commander there, Major-General Yamada, because he felt all his reserves would be needed to support the Second Army on the plain. Yamada, whose force was under constant Russian shelling, therefore decided to abandon the position after nightfall. Before he could do so, the 36th East Siberian Regiment, which had infiltrated across the river in small groups without being observed, attacked One-Tree Hill from the rear just at night fell, and took the position.

Once again poor Russian communications created problems. There were no telephone lines between the three forces involved, so the 22nd attacked, not knowing the position had already been taken. In the darkness neither force realised that those firing were not Japanese, and each returned fire. While the Russians were fighting each other, the Japanese survivors of the first attack recovered some of their positions.

At the other end of the ridge the 5th East Siberians (Major-General Putilov) attacked with two regiments (19th and 20th East Siberian Rifles) and overran the Japanese defenders on the more westerly hill within two hours. However, they did not learn until about 11.00 pm that the Japanese still held part of One-Tree Hill. Putilov organised an attack by what was left of 36th Regiment, and by dawn on 17 October the Russians had taken the whole ridge, along with 14 Japanese field guns.

So ended the battle of the Sha-Ho. The Russians lost 10,959 killed or missing, and 30,392 wounded, the Japanese less than half that number, 3,951 killed and 16,394 wounded. However, Russia's ability to replace losses was far greater than Japan's.

Kuropatkin used the recapture of the ridge to claim the battle of Sha-Ho a victory. Manifestly it was no such thing; his decision to make the main thrust in the mountains had nullified his advantages in artillery and cavalry, so his offensive had come to nothing, and his losses had been more than double those of the Japanese. However, the Russian public did not know of this effective failure, and it suited Nicholas to go along with the charade. Putilov was decorated, the tsar permitted the northerly hill to become Putilov Hill, and One-Tree Hill to be renamed Novgorod Hill, after the garrison town of the 22nd Division. Neither designation meant anything to the Chinese or Japanese. Nor could the conferring of these empty honours disguise the fact that Port Arthur must now inevitably fall. Nogi's Third Army would then be free to come north.

Nicholas may even have believed Kuropatkin's claim of a victory, because on 25 October he ended the division of powers between Kuropatkin and Alexeyev by dismissing Alexeyev, and giving Kuropatkin the full military authority he desired. Ironically, on the very next day Kuropatkin showed his real view of his 'victory' in a memorandum he sent to all unit commanders, denouncing the troops as untrained and unskilled and senior officers as incompetent, if not traitorous.

The winter lull

Although the Japanese could reasonably claim to have won at Sha-Ho, they had come closer to defeat than in any of the previous battles and the state of their ammunition and manpower precluded any immediate attempt to exploit their success. Like the Russians, they settled in for the winter.

Both sides arranged their winter quarters mainly at the expense of the local Chinese, but they differed greatly in the manner of their exploitation. In the area between the Sha and Hun rivers, the Russians completely demolished all the Chinese villages, taking the timber from them to provide roofs and walls for their underground bunkers, cutting down the fruit trees and bushes for firewood, requisitioning all the poultry, livestock and grain, and making at least 90,000 Chinese penniless refugees in their own country. Between the Hun river and Mukden they left the villages standing, but then regularly raided them for food, drink, fuel or sex. In the cities drunkenness abounded, venereal diseases were common enough, especially among officers, for Kuropatkin to issue diatribes about them, and smallpox was rampant.

The Japanese too inflicted hardships on the Chinese, requisitioning their homes and obliging them to double-up in houses not requisitioned, but the houses were not destroyed. Army regulations about cleanliness and the Japanese liking for hot baths usually led to the construction of simple bath-houses and to attempts to improve drainage, sanitation and roads. In the larger cities Japanese officers were appointed as civil governors, and worked closely with the local Chinese administration. Their main function was to protect the soldiers' health by improving sanitation and ensuring daily checks of brothels by army medical officers. In at least one city, Mukden, they provided a

The Russian battleship, Retvizan, before the war.

free hospital for Chinese civilians, and in several cities and many villages troops were used to improve roads. Japanese troops were in any case less given to leaving their billets when off duty, their rations more adequate and more regularly provided than in the Russian Army, and they were accustomed to cooking them in their billets; so their presence was less obvious and therefore less irritating to the locals than that of Russian troops. The Chinese did not exactly welcome either foreign presence, but the Japanese gave them less to complain of, and this paid off in a greater readiness among the Chinese to provide information about Russian movements and actions.

The fall of Port Arthur

The focus now turned back to Port Arthur. In mid-November the 11-in Krupp howitzers arrived from Japan and were hauled from the railhead, eight miles (13km) from the city, by teams of soldiers, 800 to a gun, to previously prepared concrete emplacements. Thousands of 500lb (227 kilo) shells also arrived. For Nogi the obvious targets for these powerful, though not especially accurate, guns were the Russian fortifications, but the navy also had an interest. While the warships in Port Arthur remained capable of moving, Togo had to stay in the vicinity; but with the 2nd Pacific Squadron now known to be well on its way, he wanted to take his ships back to Japan for repair and overhaul. Hits by the 11-in guns would immobilise the ships in the harbour, and Togo could then depart for Sasebo.

The Japanese had no observation point that overlooked the entire harbour, and the Russians, knowing this, kept moving the ships. West of the town a mountain known to the Russians as Vysokaya (High), and to the Japanese as 203-Metre Hill, provided the observation point the Japanese needed. But so far Nogi had shown little awareness of its potential.

It was policy to publish only good news of the war, and there was none from Port Arthur, so nothing was published. Inevitably this gave rise to rumours of disaster. Dissatisfaction with Nogi grew. The Chief-of-General-Staff, Marshal Yamagata, wanted to replace him, but the emperor refused his consent. Marshal Oyama wanted to replace Nogi with Kodama, his own Chief-of-Staff and the acknowledged mastermind of his campaign. He sent Kodama to Port Arthur, where Nogi did everything Kodama told him to do, so it proved unnecessary to replace him. Kodama concentrated the efforts of Third Army, now strengthened by the newly arrived 7th Division (General Oseko), on taking 203-Metre Hill. As usual with Kodama, the assault on it was to be combined with diversionary assaults elsewhere, in this case the line of forts along the so-called Chinese Wall.

The defence of 203-Metre Hill was under the same Colonel Tretyakov who had distinguished himself at Nan-shan; he had five companies of infantry, some sailor machine-gunners, some engineer troops and an artillery battery. Against them Nogi sent the entire 1st Division and parts of two other divisions, with strong artillery support, including four of the 11-in howitzers. The hill, and the adjacent Akasaka Yama, changed sides several times between 27 November and 4 December. Finally Tretyakov was seriously wounded, and by the evening of 5 December 203-Metre Hill was in Japanese hands. The cost to the Japanese was 14,000 dead, including almost all of 7th Division; the Russians had over 5,000 dead. An observation post was placed on the hill on 6 December, and in two days shells from the siege guns directed from the hill had all the battleships except the *Sevastopol* sitting on the mud of the harbour bottom.

Togo now set about destroying *Sevastopol* by torpedo attacks; over the next three weeks 120 torpedoes were fired at her. Protected by booms and nets she was badly damaged, but not destroyed. Of the 35 ships which attacked her, two were sunk, six others were damaged, and the cruiser *Takasago* went down to a mine. Rear-Admiral Viren sent his remaining destroyers out in the hope that they might escape, but all were captured or interned.

After the fall of 203-Metre Hill Stessel held a council of war. Smirnov argued that the fortress could hold out till at least mid-January, and Stessel ordered it defended to the last. But on 15 December Smirnov's most dogged supporter, General Kondratenko, was killed. Over Smirnov's objections Stessel appointed Fok in his place, and on 29 December Stessel called another council of war. The majority favoured holding out, but a minority, headed by Fok, favoured surrender. Stessel ostensibly accepted the majority opinion, but had already notified Nicholas that surrender was imminent. In the next few days the Japanese captured four of the forts on the Chinese Wall, and on 1 January 1905 Stessel asked Nogi for surrender terms. The surrender was

signed on 2 January, and the garrison, 878 officers, 23,491 solders and 8,956 sailors, laid down their arms. There were also about 15,000 wounded and sick (mostly with scurvy) in the hospitals. That night Captain von Essen took the *Sevastopol* to sea and scuttled it, before he and his crew rowed back to harbour and surrendered.

Nogi's terms were generous. Civilians could leave, and officers were given a choice. They could either become prisoners of war with their men, or give their parole to take no further part in the war and return to Russia. When the troops heard of the surrender, all shreds of discipline vanished, and they embarked on a looting

spree. The Japanese celebrated victory more decorously round their camp fires outside town. Both the Japanese and the war correspondents were shocked at the behaviour of paroled Russian officers, who pushed civilians, mostly women and children, aside in order to get the best seats on the first train to leave Port Arthur since the previous May.

Winter cavalry raids

Kuropatkin now had three armies, the First, Second and Third Manchurian, commanded by Linevich, Grippenberg and Kaulbars

respectively. By December he had received ample reinforcements and supplies, and though the surrender of Port Arthur was a setback, it had long been expected. At least he was now rid of pressures for offensives to relieve it. However, this also meant that Nogi's Third Army would soon come north, and that raised the question of impeding its transfer by cutting the South Manchurian Railway behind the Japanese lines. The obvious answer was to use his hitherto underemployed Cossacks to raid deep into the Japanese rear.

Russian dead at 203-Metre Hill. Russian soldiers collect cartridges from the dead before burial.

Handover at Port Arthur. Japanese sentries replace the Russians.

On 4 January 1905 Kuropatkin suggested a cavalry raid on Newchwang Port by General Mishchenko's Cossack Corps, a little over 7,500 strong, to destroy railway bridges and culverts. For lack of maps the corps failed to find the bridges, and the damage it did (two trains wrecked, some Japanese supplies destroyed, and telegraph and telephone lines cut) was small for the size of force. Another raid in March, by a force about 400 strong, cut some lines, destroyed a telegraph pole or two, and slightly damaged a bridge – it was repaired within hours.

The Japanese also attempted cavalry raids against the railway in the Russian rear. Two detachments from Major-General Akiyama's 1st Cavalry Brigade, one of 172 men, the

ABOVE: Russian and Japanese fraternise.

BELOW: Port Arthur shortly before surrender, with houses damaged by shelling, and sunken warships sitting on the bottom of the harbour.

other of 104, were sent off in January to make wide detours through neutral Mongolia, then turn into Manchuria to attack the South Manchurian Railway and move through Mongolia again to attack the Chinese Eastern Railway between Harbin and Tsitsihar. They found the railways too strongly guarded to do more than destroy some telegraph poles and rails and slightly damage a bridge.

Kuropatkin's new army commanders soon began adding to his troubles. Grippenberg first advocated an offensive to encircle the Japanese Second Army, and when Kuropatkin rejected it as too ambitious, he swung to extreme pessimism and, supported by Kaulbars, advocated retreating to Harbin. Both viewed the imminent arrival of Nogi with apprehension; they would probably have been even more apprehensive had they known that Oyama and Kodama thought Nogi incompetent. Kodama wanted the entire Third Army headquarters replaced before the move north, but given the difficulty of demoting the general who had just taken Port Arthur, he settled for replacing his Chief-of-Staff.

The battle of San-de-pu

Grippenberg and Kaulbars finally agreed to attack before the Third Army arrived, and Kuropatkin issued orders on 19 January for the Second Manchurian Army to drive south-west from the Hun to the Tai-tsu river at Liaoyang and outflank the Japanese Second Army. The outcome was the battle known as San-de-pu or Hei-kou-tai, two fortified villages at the western end of the Japanese line. San-de-pu, the larger, was just west of the Hun river, about 30 miles south-west of Mukden.

Despite the increased Russian strength, the old faults were apparent. The Japanese knew what was coming, and moved to counter it. Kuropatkin afterwards blamed this on premature moves by Grippenberg, but it is more likely that poor Russian security blew the plan beforehand; and, had he really believed what he said, would he not have changed his plan?

Oyama reinforced his left flank, and when the 1st Siberian Rifle Corps attacked Hei-kou-tai on 25 January it took it only at enormous cost. The 14th Division, which was meant to attack San-de-pu at the same time, failed to do so because of faulty information; when finally it did attack, a day late, it chose the wrong village, Pao-tai-tzu, and was mown down by fire from San-de-pu, about 600 yards away. Shtakelberg, was dismissed. The fiasco further demoralised the Russians, and erupted into scandal when Grippenberg declared himself ill, decamped, and on his way to St Petersburg stopped at Harbin to denounce Kuropatkin as a traitor.

Despite the failure at San-de-pu, Kuropatkin awaited spring with confidence. His eastern flank, in the mountains south-east of Mukden, was defended by the First Manchurian Army, under Linevich. In the centre was the Third Manchurian, now commanded by Bilderling; on the right, the Second Manchurian, where Kaulbars had replaced Grippenberg. The Russians totalled 275,000 infantry, 16,000 cavalry and 1,439 guns, in 369 infantry battalions and 117 cavalry squadrons, up till then the biggest force ever assembled under one commander.

The Japanese confronted them with five armies, from east to west the Yalu Army (General Kawamura); the First (Kuroki); Fourth (Nozu); Second (Oku); and Third (Nogi). A Japanese Army was much smaller than a Russian one, however, and between them the five mustered a little under 200,000 infantry, 7,350 cavalry and 924 guns, in 248 infantry battalions and 58 cavalry squadrons, outweighing the Russians only in machine guns, at 174 to 56.

Cossacks. Much was expected of them, but they proved almost useless.

The battle of Mukden

The Japanese plan

Oyama and Kodama knew they were
outnumbered, so as at Liaoyang, reacted by
moving quickly. Third Army's last units
arrived from Port Arthur on 19 February and
Oyama issued his battle orders the next day.
The Yalu Army was in terrain which made
either a rapid or a surprise advance too
difficult, so it was instead given the opening
role of attacking the Russians' left (east) wing,
to distract their attention while Third Army
launched the real main thrust, an outflanking
movement against their western flank.

The Russian plan

Kuropatkin issued his orders on 21 February,
basically repeats of those for San-de-pu. They
were compiled in ignorance of Third Army's
presence opposite his right wing, and of the
Yalu Army attacks as merely diversionary.
Second Manchurian Army was to blast its
way through Japanese Second, starting on
24 February. As Oyama hoped he would,
Kuropatkin took the Yalu Army attack as the
main Japanese thrust, perhaps misled by the
appearance on its sector of 11th Division,
transferred from Third Army. Kuropatkin
concluded that the Third Army was all there,
and so sent his reserve of 42 battalions and
128 guns to reinforce his eastern wing, He
also feared that the Japanese had learned
of his plan to attack their western wing,
and on 24 February he asked Kaulbars
whether he thought the planned offensive
should go ahead. Kaulbars asked for
reinforcement from the reserve, but when
told they had all gone to the eastern sector,
he declined to attack; yet again a Russian
offensive was stifled at birth.

Kuropatkin's erroneous belief was fortified
when Kuroki's First Army began attacking
on 25 February on Yalu Army's left.
On 27 February Oyama's intentions became
clearer. Third Army crossed the Hun river
and began advancing north between the
Hun and Liao rivers, beyond the end of the
Russian line, while Fourth Army opened a
bombardment with 108 guns, including

six 11-in Krupp howitzers brought from
Port Arthur. They were not very accurate, but
realisation of their presence caused a drop
in Russian morale disproportionate to the
few casualties they inflicted.

Learning of Nogi's outflanking movement
shortly before midday, Kaulbars sent
two Cossack detachments to counter it, but
because most of the Russian cavalry had
been sent east, he could not adequately
challenge Third Army while simultaneously
blocking Second Army's attacks. His
thoughts began to turn to retreat, and so
did those of Bilderling, with his defences
on the Putilov and Novgorod hills under
constant bombardment by Fourth Army's
demoralising siege guns.

Having sent all his reserves to the wrong
sector, Kuropatkin could only cobble
together a force to counter Nogi by breaking
up the Second Manchurian Army. He gave
Kaulbars charge of the ad hoc force, but its
attempt to redeploy was severely hampered
by a blizzard on 2 March. On the eastern
sector ammunition supplies failed to get
through on 3 March, and the Japanese
exploited the shortage to storm the
dominant hill in the Russian defences.
Rennenkampf recovered part of it only by
using all available men, including bandsmen,
cooks and clerks.

The supply dumps behind the armies and
in Mukden were ordered destroyed, to keep
them out of Japanese hands. As the word
spread, the troops rushed to loot their large
vodka stocks. On 3 March Kuropatkin
ordered Kaulbars to attack the next morning,
but Kaulbars reported inability to do so until
5 March. On that morning he made the final
attempt to save Mukden, with 48 battalions,
under General Gerngross, on the right,
44 battalions on the left, and 199 guns
in support.

The Japanese position was not entirely
satisfactory. Nogi's advance north-west of
Mukden had slowed down considerably, but
he was far ahead of the Second and Fourth
Armies, with orders to advance east of
Mukden, then wheel towards Third Army in
a pincer movement. The distance between

Battle of Mukden

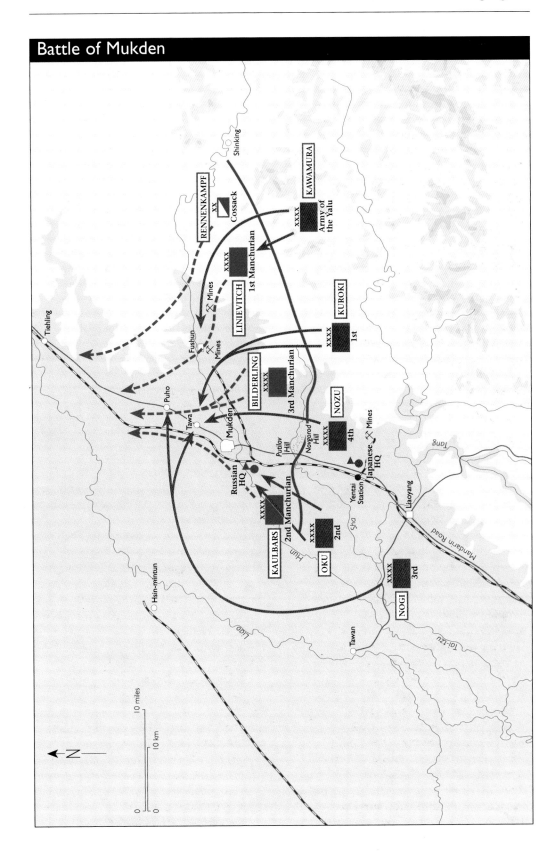

the two pincers meant neither could support the other if Kaulbars attacked in force, as he now intended to do. To remedy this, Second Army transferred its most easterly division to Fourth Army, received a replacement from general reserve and during the night of 5/6 March crossed the Hun to come up on Third Army's right. On 7 March the railway north of Mukden was cut, prompting Kuropatkin to send a dramatic telegram to St Petersburg: 'I am surrounded.' In fact the line had been cut only by a Third Army patrol, and communication was soon restored. Nevertheless Kuropatkin now saw abandonment of Mukden as the only way to save his armies, so he ordered Second and Third Manchurian Armies to withdraw after nightfall behind strong rearguards.

Noting on 7 March that Kaulbars' offensive was half-hearted, and that the Russians facing First Army were withdrawing, Oyama ordered a general attack for the next morning. But at 9.00 pm news came that the Russian withdrawal was general, so the order was changed to pursuit. First Army was to start at midnight, Fourth at 3.00 am on 8 March, the others as soon as possible, with the aim of turning the retreat into a rout.

At 6.45 pm on 9 March Kuropatkin ordered a retreat to Tieh-ling, about 40 miles (64 km) north of Mukden. That day and well into the next a dust storm of exceptional fury raged, augmented by smoke from the burning supply dumps and punctuated by explosions from burning ammunition and, finally, the blowing-up of bridges.

The retreat was disorderly, as the Japanese periodically cut the railway and road and had to be driven off, and many casualties were incurred as they fired on the Russians from both sides into the narrow escape corridor. Some troops lost their way and were killed or captured, and hundreds of carts loaded with ammunition, food and personal belongings were lost Discipline in many units collapsed, the men turning on their officers, stealing their possessions and transport, and fleeing. But Oyama did not achieve his rout. This was probably due more to the exhaustion of the Japanese infantry

than to shortcomings of its generals, but yet again decisive victory eluded them.

The battle exacted a heavy price from both sides and cost each almost a third of its force. The Japanese lost 15,892 dead and 59,612 wounded, the Russians over 40,000 killed, missing or captured, and over 49,000 wounded. It had been the biggest battle of all time until then, though later technologies of warfare would see its slaughter surpassed many times in the world wars.

Kuropatkin did not linger at Tieh-ling. With much of his transport and supplies lost and Russian morale at rock bottom, it seemed prudent to put a respectable distance between himself and the Japanese. He torched Tieh-ling and retreated to Hsi-ping-kai, 200 miles (320 km) to the north. Nicholas dismissed him as Commander-in-Chief, but granted his plea to command an army, so he and Linevich changed places. The Japanese took Mukden and followed the Russians, but not closely. They, too, had had enough of fighting for the present.

Confusion at sea

In St Petersburg Rear-Admiral Rozhestvensky battled for months to turn the Baltic Fleet into the 2nd Pacific Squadron. He announced that it would sail on 15 July 1904, but three more months passed before it left. The biggest problem was how to get enough coal for a voyage of 18,000 nautical miles. Russia had no coaling stations abroad and could expect no British cooperation; France would allow only limited refuelling at its colonial ports. Kaiser Wilhelm II, who welcomed Russia's Far East entanglement because it distracted it from European affairs, was more helpful, but had only one colony, South-West Africa, on the route. However, he arranged for 60 colliers of the Hamburg–Amerika line to meet the fleet at various points.

The main striking force consisted of four new sister battleships – *Knyaz Suvorov* (flagship), *Imperator Alexander III, Borodino* and *Orel* – and three older and slower battleships, *Oslyabya*, *Sisoy Veliky* and *Navarin*. They were accompanied by four modern and three older cruisers and nine destroyers, and supported by a fleet of auxiliaries, including a repair ship, *Kamchatka*, a hospital ship, tugs and other support vessels, a total force of more than 50 ships, needing about half a million tons of coal.

The voyage began inauspiciously, with two of the new battleships running aground, *Orel* at Kronstadt and *Suvorov* at the Baltic port of Libava, which the squadron left on 15 October, amid rumours that Japanese destroyers, torpedo boats and even submarines were lurking in the North Sea. Some of these reports may have been spread by Colonel Akashi and his agents. Others seem to have originated with agents recruited by the Russians, unskilled in identifying ships, but eager to have the money paid for information; behind them was the knowledge that almost all Japanese warships were British-built, so the Japanese Navy were not strangers to the North Sea. Before it had even left Danish waters, the *Kamchatka*, lost in fog, radioed that it was being attacked by eight torpedo boats; after 20 minutes' silence it reported that it could not see any boats, but the incident served to create a high level of anxiety and led to the Dogger Bank incident, in which the squadron fired on British trawlers and sank one. This temporarily brought the two countries close to war, but was resolved by a Russian apology and compensation, though Rozhestvensky and his officers ever after asserted that torpedo boats had been lurking among the trawlers, or had even been disguised as fishing boats. British cruisers shadowed the squadron past Gibraltar, bringing morale down still further by demonstrating seamanship beyond anything of which the Russians were capable.

The voyage was both odyssey and ordeal. The ships, overloaded, with coal stowed in every available space, survived numerous breakdowns, wallowed through a hurricane off the Cape of Good Hope, and reached Nossi-be in Madagascar to the news of the surrender at Port Arthur and the massacre of demonstrators at the Winter Palace in St Petersburg on 'Bloody Sunday', 22 January 1905. Unrest spread through the fleet, culminating in a mutiny in the cruiser *Nakhimov*. It was forcibly suppressed, and 14 sailors were executed. Rozhestvensky's decision to send home one of his oldest ships, the *Malay*, with the worst troublemakers and some of the most seriously ill, almost misfired, when the prisoners seized control of the ship. Fortunately for him, the ship was just leaving harbour, and a boarding party from the flagship managed to regain control. The older ships, which he had sent via the Suez Canal, rejoined the squadron, but a new problem arose over coal.

The Hamburg–Amerika line had so far faithfully fulfilled its contract, but soon after the squadron's arrival in Madagascar the Japanese protested forcefully that its presence in a French colony was a breach of neutrality, and announced that any colliers found near the squadron would be sunk. The Hamburg–Amerika line then told Rozhestvensky that it could provide no further supplies, but he resolved the situation by threatening an expensive damages suit and buying 10 of the colliers on his government's behalf. The company then agreed to have four ships rendezvous with the squadron at Saigon, in French Indo-China (now Vietnam), but would go no closer to the theatre of war.

To add to his problems of tropical disease, suicide and discontent among his crews, Rozhestvensky faced interference from a well-connected, self-appointed naval strategist, Captain Nicholas Klado, who had contrived to have himself appointed to Rozhestvensky's staff but whom the admiral managed to get rid of by sending him home to testify at the enquiry into the Dogger Bank incident. Back in St Petersburg, Klado induced the admiralty to form the 3rd Pacific Squadron, from ships that Rozhestvensky had rejected as old, slow or outdated. This squadron, comprising the old battleship *Tsar Nikolay I*, the cruiser *Vladimir Monomakh*

The Dogger Bank incident, 22 October 1904.

(originally built as a sailing frigate) and the coastal defence monitors *Apraksin*, *Ushakov* and *Senyavin*, and commanded by Rear-Admiral Nikolay Nebogatov, was on its way, and Rozhestvensky was to await its arrival. Noting that this would add no real strength to his squadron, while giving Togo still more time to refit his ships, Rozhestvensky offered his resignation, but Nicholas rejected it. The 2nd Pacific Squadron left Madagascar on 16 March 1905, and passed Singapore on 8 April. Among the thousands who watched it were newspaper reporters and Japanese spies, so Togo soon knew where his enemy was, and could easily calculate how long he had for preparing to meet him.

In fact he had more time than expected, because Rozhestvensky was ordered to wait at Cam Ranh Bay for the 3rd Squadron. Rozhestvensky, who categorised Nebogatov's old ships as 'self-sinkers' wanted to disobey orders and leave immediately after refuelling, but then found that *Alexander III*, which throughout the voyage had won prizes for fastest refuelling, had either miscalculated or exaggerated its stocks, and had not enough coal to reach Vladivostok; the squadron would have to wait for more coal to be delivered. Nebogatov's ships arrived on 9 May and, after coaling, the combined squadron left on 14 May.

The battle of Tsushima

They did not reach the vicinity of Japan till late May, seven and a half months after departing the Baltic. Togo had had ample time to repair his ships, and his cruisers were

about 3.30 am on 27 May, when the armed merchant cruiser *Shinano Maru* sighted the two brightly lit hospital ships at the rear of the squadron and radioed its position and course. Now certain that the Russians were heading for the western passage, at 5.00 am Togo took his four battleships and 11 cruisers to sea. The weather was too rough for torpedo attacks, so the destroyers and torpedo boats were ordered to shelter in the strait between the two islands of Tsushima and await orders.

Rozhestvensky's ships were arranged in three divisions: 1st, *Suvorov*, *Alexander III*, *Borodino* and *Orel*, approximately equalled Togo's four in fire power; 2nd, with the three older battleships, *Oslyabya*, *Sisoy Veliky* and *Navarin*, and the armoured cruiser *Nakhimov* (its commander, Admiral Felkerzam, had died two days previously, but for fear the news might affect already low morale, Rozhestvensky had kept his death a secret, even from Nebogatov); and 3rd Division, which comprised Nebogatov's old ships, *Nikolay I*, *Apraxin*, *Senyavin* and *Ushakov*, and the even older *Vladimir Monomakh*.

The balance of fire power was roughly as follows.

		Russians	Japanese
Guns	10–12 in	41	17
	8–9 in	8	30
Max speed (knots)		14–18	17–20

Thus the Russians had the edge in fire power, the Japanese in speed. Rozhestvensky's ships were overloaded with coal, and his decision to keep four transports with the squadron restricted his speed still further, to 9–11 knots. To increase his speed advantage, Togo lightened his ships by ordering most of their coal thrown overboard.

Togo planned to alternate daylight attacks by the battleships and cruisers with night attacks by the destroyers and torpedo boats over the whole distance to Vladivostok, and one flotilla of destroyers laid mines on the Russians' expected course. Before putting to sea he summoned his subordinate admirals and ships' captains and told them how he

scouting. With Port Arthur fallen, Rozhestvensky had only one possible destination, Vladivostok, but a choice of three routes to reach it, two east of Japan, then through either the La Perouse (Soya) Strait between Hokkaido and Sakhalin or the Tsugaru Strait between Hokkaido and Honshu, the third west of Japan, through the Straits of Tsushima. Togo gambled that the Russians, after their long voyage, would take the latter, being the shortest route, so stationed his battleships and most of his cruisers at Masan Bay on the Korean south coast, away from busy shipping lanes. On 25 May he received a report that six Russian auxiliaries, including colliers, had arrived at Shanghai. Rozhestvensky's sending the colliers away confirmed that he meant to take the shortest route; the only remaining uncertainty was whether he would pass west or east of Tsushima. This was resolved at proposed to conduct the battle. Rozhestvensky had done none of these things, nor even devised any tactical plan. There had been very little gunnery practice during the voyage, because of the need to conserve ammunition. Only once had the entire squadron practised a manoeuvre; that was on the previous day and was neither fully executed nor evaluated afterwards. Rozhestvensky did not trust his subordinates, and intended to direct each division by flag signals. The cruisers' ability to act as the fleet's eyes and ears was reduced by his relegating two of them to guarding the transports and another two to the task of helping any battleship that suffered damage; his few destroyers were ordered only to take off the admirals and their staffs if any flagship was disabled. In short, insofar as he had any plan, it was entirely defensive.

During the night of 26/27 May, as Flag-Captain Clapier de Colongue later recalled, 'hardly anyone slept; it was too clear we'd be meeting the enemy in full strength … Throughout the ship separate groups of the crew stood or lay, conversing quietly. The orderlies secretly tell the officers that rats have appeared on the accommodation deck.'

At about 6.00 am the cruiser *Ural* signalled that four unidentified ships had appeared behind the column. At 6.45 am Rozhestvensky was told that another ship had appeared. This was identified as the Japanese cruiser *Izumi*, and *Suvorov* turned its rear 12-in turret towards the intruder; simultaneously all the ships broke out their ensigns. Believing they were about to open fire, *Izumi* sheered away; but the flags were not battle ensigns, merely hoisted to mark the anniversary of Nicholas' coronation.

At 9.45 am, when the Russians were abreast of the southern Tsushima island, the Japanese 3rd Division (Rear-Admiral Kataoka), comprising the old ex-Chinese battleship *Chin Yen* and three cruisers, began shadowing them at a distance of 65–75 cables (a cable being 600 ft, one-tenth of a nautical mile). *Orel* opened fire, and Kataoka's ships moved away. Realising that

the rest of Togo's fleet must be nearby, Rozhestvensky ordered his ships into battle order in line abreast. While the manoeuvre was under way, Kataoka's squadron reappeared, and Rozhestvensky cancelled it; collisions were narrowly averted, and the force remained in two columns in line ahead, the 1st Division to starboard (right) of the 2nd and 3rd.

Togo intended to attack the weaker 2nd and 3rd Divisions, but when he sighted the Russians, he was ahead of them, closer to the more powerful and faster battleships of the 1st Division, and heading south. If he adhered to his plan, the 1st Division might escape, so he brought the six cruisers of his 2nd Division into line behind the four battleships and two cruisers of the 1st Division, then all 12 ships, headed by *Mikasa*, turned through 90 degrees and headed due west across the Russians' path.

It would now be relatively simple to turn all the ships and steam across the Russian front, concentrating a deadly fire on the leading ship in each column in the classic manoeuvre known as 'Crossing the T'. But that would bring his 2nd Division (Vice-Admiral Kamimura) into action first, and for two reasons Togo did not want that. First, he preferred to lead from the front, and second, given the Russian superiority in numbers of heavy guns, it made sense to lead with his heaviest guns rather than the smaller ones of Kamimura's cruisers. To turn the whole line in succession, however, would mean that each ship would be almost stationary for several minutes, within gun range of the Russian battleships, and as his ships would be able to open fire only one at a time, it would take about 15 minutes before the entire line was firing. Perhaps Togo also had a third reason, a belief that his adversary was incapable of seizing the opportunity the turn would present.

Whatever his reasons, Togo ordered the entire line to follow *Mikasa* in a complete semi-circle, just over three miles ahead of the Russians. They could hardly believe their eyes, or their luck, and their leading ships at once opened fire, scoring several hits, though none fatal. The Japanese gunnery was far more effective: within minutes *Suvorov* was on fire, and *Oslyabya* had an enormous hole in its side. It sank at 2.45 pm, just 20 minutes after coming under fire. The only Japanese ship put out of action was the cruiser *Asama*, the last in line, and it was back within two hours. Subsequent analysis found that the Russians scored only 1.5 hits per 100 shells fired, the Japanese, 3.2, over twice as effective. Furthermore, the accuracy of Japanese fire so disrupted the Russians' gun control that they scored no hits after the first half-hour.

Suvorov fought on until evening; Rozhestvensky, with several wounds, including a bone fragment in his brain, was taken aboard the destroyer *Buyny* before *Suvorov* sank, at about 7.00 pm. One of several British naval observers with the Japanese wrote of the sight: 'A marine Vereshchagin will have no difficulty finding subjects for his canvas', not knowing that the painter, world-famous for his depictions of the horrors of war, had died with Makarov when the *Petropavlovsk* had sunk. Soon after the *Suvorov* went down, *Borodino* blew up.

Togo's orders for the night torpedo attacks were practically invitations to suicide: the ships were to go to six cables (1,200 yards) or less from their targets before launching their torpedoes. The 58 destroyers and torpedo boats sent in obeyed him to the letter, and harassed the remnants of the Russian fleet, now commanded by Nebogatov, from point-blank range. By morning only two battleships, *Nikolay I* and *Orel*, were together, with the cruiser *Izumrud* and two of the old coast defence monitors.

During the night the battleships *Navarin* and *Sisoy Veliky* had ceased to fight, the first scuttled, the second surrendered, and Admiral Enkvist, though later claiming to have first made several unsuccessful attempts to break through northwards, had turned south, taking the cruisers *Oleg*, *Avrora* and *Zhemchug* to Manila and internment.

Nebogatov's situation was hopeless. Vladivostok was over 300 miles (480 km) away, *Orel* had been boarded by the Japanese, and was being towed by *Asama* to Sasebo. His flagship, *Nikolay I*, was in little better state, and the Japanese completely surrounded his ships. After consulting his staff, he decided to surrender, and hoisted a large white tablecloth; then, because the Japanese continued firing, Japanese flags. Only when his ships stopped their engines did Togo order a cease-fire and send a boat to bring Nebogatov to *Mikasa*.

Buyny, with Rozhestvensky and hundreds of survivors from *Suvorov* and *Oslyabya* on board, suffered engine failure on 29 May and the admiral was transferred to another destroyer, *Bedovy*. He was unconscious when a Japanese destroyer overhauled *Bedovy* and ordered it to stop. The Japanese captain came aboard, expressed surprise when told of Rozhestvensky's presence, and insisted on seeing him. He did not disturb him, but posted a sentry at his cabin door, and took *Bedovy* in tow to Sasebo. There Rozhestvensky was taken to hospital, where a few weeks later Togo visited him, commiserated, and shook hands. The young officer who accompanied Togo, Lieutenant Isoroku Yamamoto, 36 years later commanded the Combined Fleet and master-minded the surprise attack on Pearl Harbor.

Russian losses					
	Left Baltic	Sunk	Captured	Interned	To Vladivostok
Battleships	8	5	3	0	0
Cruisers	10	4	1	4	1
Destroyers	9	5	1	1	2
Coastal Monitors	3	0	3	0	0
Repair ships	1	1	0	0	0
Transports	6	3	0	3	0
Hospital ships	2	0	2	0	0

Battle of Tsushima

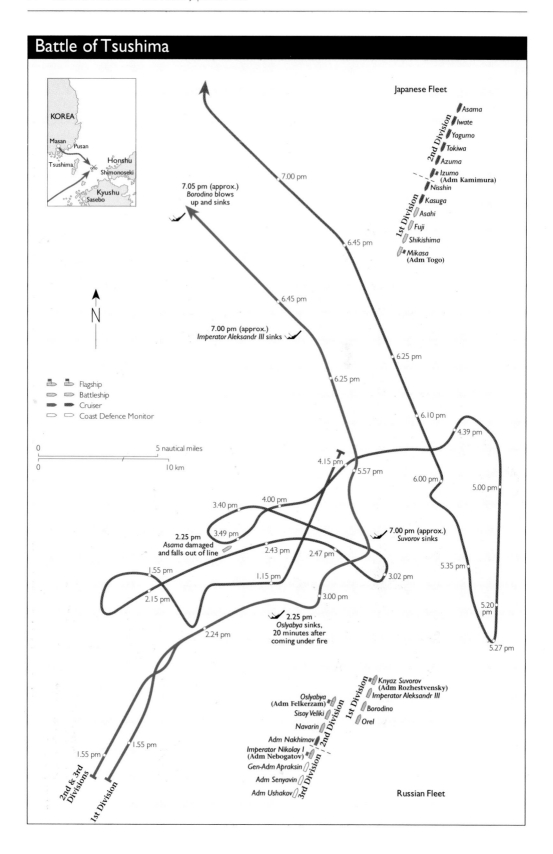

Japanese Fleet

2nd Division:
Asama
Iwate
Yagumo
Tokiwa
Azuma
Izumo (Adm Kamimura)

1st Division:
Nisshin
Kasuga
Asahi
Fuji
Shikishima
Mikasa (Adm Togo)

KOREA
Masan
Pusan
Tsushima
Honshu
Shimonoseki
Kyushu
Sasebo

7.05 pm (approx.)
Borodino blows up and sinks

7.00 pm

6.45 pm

6.45 pm

7.00 pm (approx.)
Imperator Aleksandr III sinks

6.25 pm

6.25 pm

6.10 pm

4.39 pm

5.00 pm

6.00 pm

5.35 pm

5.20 pm

5.27 pm

7.00 pm (approx.)
Suvorov sinks

3.02 pm

3.00 pm

N

Flagship
Battleship
Cruiser
Coast Defence Monitor

0   5 nautical miles
0   10 km

4.15 pm

5.57 pm

3.40 pm   4.00 pm

3.49 pm

2.25 pm
Asama damaged and falls out of line

2.43 pm   2.47 pm

1.55 pm

1.15 pm

2.15 pm

2.24 pm

2.25 pm
Oslyabya sinks, 20 minutes after coming under fire

1.55 pm

1.55 pm

1.55 pm

2nd & 3rd Divisions

1st Division

1st Division:
Knyaz Suvorov (Adm Rozhestvensky)
Imperator Aleksandr III
Borodino
Orel

2nd Division:
Oslyabya (Adm Felkerzam)
Sisoy Veliki
Navarin
Adm Nakhimov

3rd Division:
Imperator Nikolay I (Adm Nebogatov)
Gen-Adm Apraksin
Adm Senyavin
Adm Ushakov

Russian Fleet

Voyage of squadron to Port Arthur

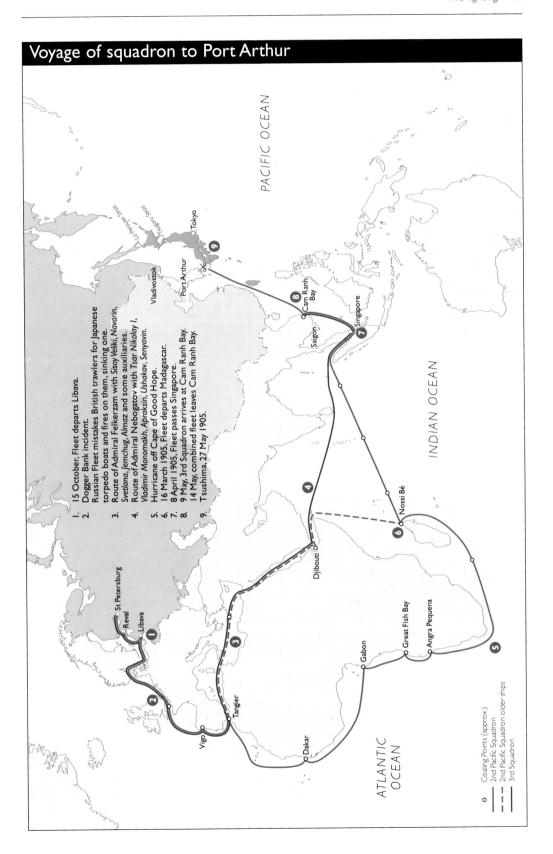

1. 15 October, Fleet departs Libava.
2. Dogger Bank incident.
   Russian Fleet mistakes British trawlers for Japanese torpedo boats and fires on them, sinking one.
3. Route of Admiral Felkerzam with *Sisoy Veliki, Navarin, Svetlana, Jemchug, Almaz* and some auxiliaries.
4. Route of Admiral Nebogatov with *Tsar Nikolay I, Vladimir Monomakh, Apraksin, Ushakov, Senyavin.*
5. Hurricane off Cape of Good Hope.
6. 16 March 1905, Fleet departs Madagascar.
7. 8 April 1905, Fleet passes Singapore.
8. 9 May, 3rd Squadron arrives at Cam Ranh Bay.
   14 May, combined fleet leaves Cam Ranh Bay.
9. Tsushima, 27 May 1905.

PACIFIC OCEAN

INDIAN OCEAN

ATLANTIC OCEAN

La Pérouse Strait
Tsugaru Strait
Tokyo
Vladivostok
Port Arthur
Cam Ranh Bay
Saigon
Singapore
Nossi Bé
Djibouti
St Petersburg
Reval
Libava
Tangier
Vigo
Dakar
Gabon
Great Fish Bay
Angra Pequena

o Coaling Points (approx.)
    2nd Pacific Squadron
    2nd Pacific Squadron older ships
    3rd Squadron

The Russians lost 4,830 killed, almost 7,000 captured and 1,862 interned. Japanese losses were three torpedo boats, 110 men killed and 590 wounded. It was a victory even more overwhelming than Trafalgar, and with consequences far more immediate. Napoleon was not finally disposed of till 10 years later, whereas Tsushima brought Nicholas to the negotiating table within three months.

Revolution in Russia

Russia had been restless all year. In January news of the surrender at Port Arthur had spawned a wave of protests at the incompetent conduct of the war. On 'Bloody Sunday', 22 January, police and troops fired on a peaceful demonstration in St Petersburg, killing or wounding several hundred people. Three weeks later Grand Duke Sergey, governor of Moscow and an uncle to the tsar, was blown to pieces by an assassin's bomb. Coming so soon after the disaster of Mukden, the catastrophe of Tsushima helped bring Russia to the brink of revolution. Anti-war demonstrations broke out in St Petersburg and several other cities, and unrest was stimulated by Colonel Akashi's support of subversives, including shipping thousands of rifles to nationalists and revolutionaries in Finland, the Baltic provinces and the Caucasus. In the Black Sea Fleet the crew of the battle-cruiser *Knyaz Potemkin Tavrichesky* mutinied, took over the ship, and shelled Odessa. Discipline in the rest of the fleet was so uncertain that no attempt to disable or retake the ship could be risked; its crew sailed it away to internment in Romania.

The tsar faced conflicting advice after Mukden. His wife wanted the war to continue, and so did the generals in Manchuria, led by Linevich and Kuropatkin. They assured him that their armies were in excellent shape and eager to attack, while the Japanese were war-weary and lacked the will to go on fighting, but Nicholas had had such assurances before, and now could not afford to believe them.

The kaiser had until then also urged him to fight on, but first Mukden and then

Tsushima forced on Wilhelm the realisation that Nicholas' hold on power could be menaced by revolution if the war continued to go badly. This might infect Austria–Hungary or even Germany, and the reports he was receiving from German officer observers with the Russians in Manchuria painted a less rosy picture than did Nicholas's generals. So he did not query Nicholas's decision to end the war.

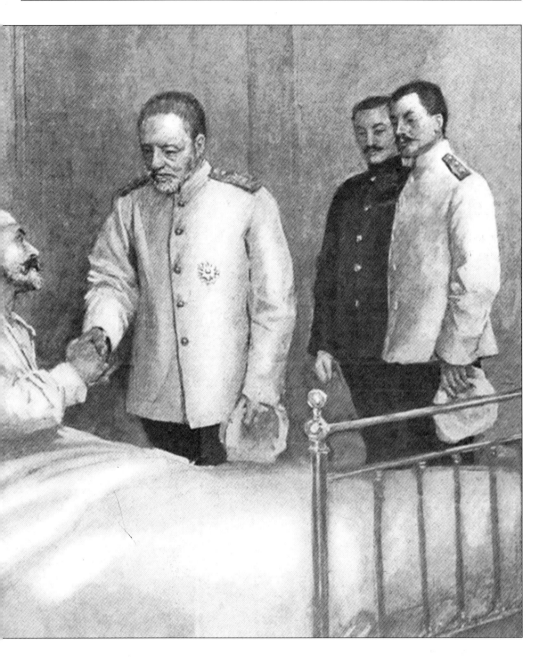

Exhaustion in Japan

Togo visiting Rozhestvensky in hospital.

Japan had already had to recognise the need to stop the war even before Tsushima. Ultra-nationalists might talk of advancing across the Urals and storming St Petersburg, but Japan's money and manpower were running low. General Kodama had arrived back in Tokyo on 28 March, less than three weeks after Mukden and two months before Tsushima, specifically to tell the emperor and government that the war must be ended, and Japan's most influential statesman, Hirobumi Ito, supported him. Even before Kodama's arrival, President Theodore Roosevelt had been approached to mediate, and on 20 March he had notified his readiness to do so. On 21 April the cabinet decided on its negotiating position, and the victory five weeks later at Tsushima gave it an additional incentive to quit while ahead.

Up till then the land war had been unusual in being fought entirely on third- party territory, China and Korea. Kodama now supported a last push to strengthen Japan's negotiating position by seizing the Russian island of Sakhalin. On 7 July Japanese troops began landing, and by 8 August, the day the formal negotiations began, they controlled the whole island. Resistance was negligible. About half the 8,000-strong defending force were convicts, induced to serve by promise of reduced sentences and virtually untrained, while their commander, General Lipanov, was, as one Japanese participant put it, 'a former lawyer, very imperfectly acquainted with military matters'. Thus ended the fighting.

Russia's harsh reality

The soldiers and sailors on both sides were overwhelmingly conscripts, but whereas most Japanese could read and write, few Russians were literate, so their experiences have to be derived mostly from diaries kept by junior officers. However, reports by the numerous foreign observers, especially the 29 British officers with the Japanese, provide a considerable amount of information on life in the ranks.

Russian soldiers shared their superiors' beliefs that beating the Japanese would be easy. ('Peace will be signed in Tokyo within three weeks of the first shot,' wrote one.) That belief evaporated after the first encounters. Among Russian sailors, however, defeatism was noted even before the war by F. T. Jane, a leading naval analyst. He wrote that the Russian seaman felt he existed to be shot at, while his British counterpart felt he existed to shoot others. One lieutenant complained that all the sailors had to be taught everything, 'half because they know nothing, the other half because they have forgotten everything'.

The sailors at Port Arthur were defeatist from the outset, except for the few short weeks of Makarov's presence; so too were many in the 2nd Squadron. (One wrote home soon after departure: 'I feel inclined to hang myself.') Many more became defeatist during the voyage, some to the extent of committing suicide, and senior officers endorsed their subordinates' pessimism. On 9 October 1904, just before the voyage began, Captain Bukhvostov, of *Alexander III*, responded to the good wishes of the tsar and admiralty: 'There will be no victory ... but we will know how to die.' After the Dogger Bank incident a young officer expressed disappointment that the British had not declared war, so that the squadron could be sunk then and there, and saved from a long voyage 'to meet the same fate'.

Conditions on board the Russian ships were appalling, as all the ships had far more coal on board than they had been designed to carry – the four new battleships, for example, with bunkers for 1,100 tons, had to carry twice that amount. Coal was stowed in the cabins of all officers up to commanders, on the mess decks where the men lived, in passages, bathrooms, drying rooms and torpedo flats, between guns, and in piles on decks. Coal dust was everywhere, and during passage around Africa combined with the heat and humidity to make life almost intolerable, causing numerous cases of heat stroke, and several deaths. One sailor wrote: 'Our lungs were choked with dust ... we swallowed it with our food ... it became a sort of black veil hiding all else.'

Mutinous conduct began off West Africa, and increased during the halts in Madagascar and Indo-China, culminating in mutinies in *Navarin* and *Malay*. There were also many self-inflicted wounds and suicides, but the lowest ebb of morale came through homesickness, when a ship thought to be bringing mail from home was found to have on board letters written by squadron members a month earlier and not yet mailed.

Japanese sailors had no cause for low morale, and displayed none. As one wrote: 'The [Russian] fear of death is unknown here.' Another said of his reaction to the decision to go to war: 'I cried ... when a man is strongly moved, he apparently cries before he rejoices.'

Japanese soldiers were equally affected by the national mood, but were initially less confident that the sailors. One described their duty in the siege of Port Arthur as that of 'human bullets'. Another likened life in the trenches to living 'in the stink of rotting flesh and crumbling bones ... like spirits with sharp, eager passions in miserable bodies'.

Unlike the Russians, who generally saw conscription as a hardship, the Japanese, then still mostly small farmers, viewed it not only as an opportunity to serve emperor and country, but as a much easier life when not actually fighting, with pay, clothing and three meals a day. In summer the Japanese soldier rose at 5.00 am, breakfasted at 6.00 am, and paraded at 7.00 am. After about three hours of drill he was free until lunch at noon, then free again until afternoon parade, which began at 3.00 pm or 4.00 pm, but which he would not be required to attend unless judged in need of special instruction. He had his third meal around 6.30 pm, and the evening was given to baths, games, gymnastics, wrestling or watching plays (always on patriotic themes, emphasising the need to give up everything, life included, if country and emperor so required). Bedtime was 9.30 pm. Soldiers judged specially efficient had to attend parade only once a week.

Despite the generous free time, the Japanese soldier usually stayed in his quarters. As one observer put it, he did 'not roam about the towns and villages as British soldiers do', but slept, wrote, smoked, drank tea and washed clothing. He was paid every ten days, and received a quarter-pint of sake every three days, and 20 cigarettes a week plus cakes and sweets, as gifts from the emperor. His staple food was rice, supplemented by fish, vegetables, meat, pickles and sauces, and extra rations were given to men in the front line or on outpost duty. The same observer noted: 'From highest to lowest, the greatest attention is paid to feeding of the men', which was considered to contribute greatly to freedom from sickness in the field, and he also mentioned that he had not seen one drunken man. Lieutenant-General Hamilton, one of the three most senior British observers, went so far as to describe the Japanese as 'the world's best infantry'.

However, letters home depicted a slightly less idyllic situation for the Japanese conscript. Complaints or descriptions of failures were lacking, probably to avoid censorship, but devotion to the state, rather than to locality or clan, was not particularly strong, and awareness of the emperor and his claimed divinity was quite low among soldiers, although stronger in the navy. In the siege of Port Arthur the regiment refusing to leave its trenches was not an isolated case. On more than one occasion military police or troops were stationed behind frontline units to prevent their running away. Even the Japanese soldier's indifference to death had its limits.

One example of the varying attitudes between the two sides is the arrangements for troops travelling by train. Russians regularly complained of receiving neither food nor water during whole days in transit. Japanese troops returning home travelled first, 800 to a train, from Tieh-ling to Dalny, a 37-hour journey. Feeding stations were erected at six points, each with two 800-seat dining halls, one to be prepared while the other was occupied. Served by tramways from the kitchen, loaded trolleys passed through the halls and empty ones returned outside them.

Observers with the Russian armies had less to say about the soldier's daily life, but reports were seldom complimentary. Relations among the soldiers were often poor; those from European Russia tended to see Siberians as stupid and unreliable, and viewed themselves as having come to rescue them; Siberians in turn, and particularly Far Easterners, accused European Russians of not taking seriously the threat that they themselves perceived from Japan. (In 1918 roles would be reversed; when the Russian Army collapsed, Siberian units were the first to decamp.)

At Port Arthur relations between the soldiers and sailors were bad, especially after the transfer of many of the ships' guns to the forts, which showed that there was no intention to take the ships to sea to fight the Japanese. One naval officer recorded that it had been suggested 'in all seriousness' that the guns of the forts open fire on the squadron 'to force it to put to sea and fight'. As in most armies of the time, infantrymen tended to envy the cavalry, but the Cossacks, of whom much was expected, ended up despised, partly because of poor performance in the field and partly because of the role Cossacks played in suppressing popular unrest in St Petersburg and other cities of European Russia.

Relations between officers and men were far more distant in the Russian than in the Japanese Army, partly because most officers came from well-to-do urban or rural aristocratic background or at least from the gentry, while most men were illiterate peasants. In contrast, most Japanese officers came from the same rural backgrounds as their men, and all were literate. Numerous foreign observers criticised Russian officers' disregard of their men's welfare, and three naval mutinies, in *Nakhimov*, *Orel* and *Potemkin*, were triggered by officers' willingness to allow bad food to be served to the men – mouldy biscuits in the first and suspect meat in the other two.

Russian defeats add to domestic unrest

The war exacerbated the strains already present in Russian society. Colonel Akashi had no difficulty in recruiting agents and arming revolutionaries in Finland, the Baltic Provinces, Poland, the Caucasus, Ukraine and Russia. Army units arrived in Manchuria under strength because of desertions en route, and lost more in the field when non-Russian conscripts, especially Poles, willingly surrendered or defected. Internationally, only Germany, and to a lesser extent France, supported Russia, while the USA, Britain and its dominions actively favoured Japan, ignoring the facts that it was the aggressor, had not pre-empted a Russian assault (since Russia had no such intent) and had attacked before declaring war. The London *Times* went so far as to describe the surprise attack on Port Arthur as destined for 'a place of honour in naval annals'. A different verdict would greet repetition of the ploy at Pearl Harbor in 1941.

The Dogger Bank incident brought calls for war in Britain, but was settled when Nicholas agreed to have an international commission investigate the incident. Accepting its findings, he paid compensation to the families of the dead and injured, and replaced the sunken fishing boat with a new one.

The war as such impacted far less directly on Russia than on Japan, but the immediate consequences were more far-reaching. The paradox was only apparent. For Russia, the war was a local one, fought at a great distance from its main centres, not substantially straining the country's manpower or material resources, and only adding marginally to already deep-seated reasons for unrest in a multi-ethnic empire; for Japan, it was a war close to home which absorbed proportionally more of its smaller population, and necessitated heavy taxation

to pay for it, in a culturally homogenous society not otherwise discontented with its lot.

Russian society, on the other hand, was in a state of unrest before the war. It was not only among non-Russian subjects such as Finns or Poles, but among Russians too that there were elements (Lenin among them) who actively welcomed the prospect of defeat for its weakening effect on Nicholas's absolutist regime. They called for increases in anti-government activity to help bring it about. There was no such subversion in Japan; even those such as Hirobumi Ito, who had opposed making war, recognised the importance of winning, and supported the war effort.

Both societies harboured Messianic self-perceptions. Influential groups in the Russian intelligentsia, whether Panslavist or Westerniser, saw Russia as a 'young' country destined to lead 'the East' (basically meaning Slavdom) to reject or emulate the 'old' West, and in either case, ultimately to supplant it. The war overturned this perception, because suddenly Russia found itself (culturally as well as geographically) the 'West' and defeated by the 'East'. Only after the Communist seizure of power in November 1917 would Russia again venture seriously to present itself as the 'wave of the future'.

Japanese Messianism naturally saw victory as glorifying 'modern' Japan; until 1945 the anniversaries of the battles of Mukden and Tsushima were celebrated as army and navy days respectively. A shrine to General Nogi, who committed ritual suicide following the death of Emperor Meiji in 1912, was erected in 1923, and one to Admiral Togo, who died in 1934, was built in 1940.

Theatre and the new art form, film, were exploited in Japan, where about 80 per cent of films produced in 1904/05 dealt with the war. Both fostered a myth in which acts of heroism, uncommon enough in real war to be rewarded by medals and promotions, were presented as the norm, and victories over superior numbers, real as they were, came to be attributed not to superior professionalism and discipline, nor the enemy's shortcomings, but to a mystical Japanese 'spirit' (*Yamato-damashii*) that could overcome any odds. In particular, the low-loss victories of the Yellow Sea and Tsushima fostered an illusion of invincibility at sea that, despite differences over priorities between army and navy, encouraged both to think of expansion to the Asian mainland and Pacific islands.

The impact on neutral China

Except for the Japanese occupation of Sakhalin at the very end, the war was unusual in not being fought on the territory of either belligerent. The casualties on both sides (31,630 Russians and 49,400 Japanese killed) were small relative to each country's population, so the war had little direct impact on the civilian population other than for relatives of the dead. Unrest in the Russian Empire long predated the war; the humiliating defeats in the first five months of 1905 (Port Arthur on 1 January, Mukden in March and Tsushima in May) aggravated but did not cause the popular dissatisfaction that expressed itself in riots in St Petersburg, Moscow, Warsaw and elsewhere. The only Russian civilians to suffer directly from the war were those resident in Port Arthur or evacuated there from Dalny. The majority, engaged in business, suffered loss of their homes and stocks of goods; they shared the garrison's hardships as food supplies dwindled, and the risk of death from the Japanese shelling. However, once the fortress surrendered, the Japanese provided trains to take civilians to Russian-held territory.

In Japan the regime enjoyed the popular support that its Russian counterpart lacked, but the high levels of taxation needed to pay for the war caused considerable hardship and resentment. Popular expectation that Russia would be made to pay for the war was disappointed by the negotiators' failure to extract an indemnity. Resentment exploded in several days of rioting in Tokyo and other cities, with burning of police boxes and many deaths, but the unrest was short-lived.

The civilians most affected by the war were neutrals, the Chinese inhabitants of Manchuria. Initially both sides tried to maintain good relations with them, but behaviour on the Russian side soon deteriorated. The city of Liaoyang had the unenviable record of being looted three times in three days. The Russians plundered the shops, mostly for food and alcohol, before they retreated. The Chinese garrison and police took anything the Russians had left. The Japanese arrived hungry, after five days fighting on handfuls of dry rice; finding no food in the twice-looted shops, they took what they wanted from private homes.

Among Russian troops the Cossacks had the worst reputation for looting, perhaps because a cavalryman could carry off more in his saddle-bags than an infantryman in his pack, but also because the frustration induced by successive defeats was taken out on the defenceless Chinese. The rationale they adopted was that of suspicion that the Chinese were helping the Japanese, whether or not they were. Some Chinese villages were destroyed to provide timber for Russian winter quarters; others were torched, their women raped and their cattle and poultry butchered. Those who resisted, or who simply did not understand what the Russians wanted, often were killed. One eyewitness noted that an entire family hiding in a pit was killed because someone suggested they were Japanese spies.

The atrocities merely intensified Chinese support for the generally less destructive, better-organised and more disciplined Japanese. A criminal element among the Chinese, well-armed bandit groups, often ex-soldiers, variously known as 'Chunguses', 'Chunchuse' or 'khunhuzy', preyed on Russian supply columns. This was partly because Colonel Aoki paid them to do so, but even when unpaid, they went after the rich booty, because Russian depredations made them more presentable as avengers among the Chinese, their normal peacetime prey, while also reducing their attacks on

Chinese. The Russians, who called them simply 'mounted bandits', did not realise that many of them were in Japanese pay. Their contribution to the war effort was marginal. They found the railways too well guarded to be attractive targets, and as the Russians fell back, their ability to rely on the railways for supply, and to guard columns of carts taking supplies from railhead to frontline units increased. Nevertheless, they had a greater impact on the Russians than on the Japanese and increased the Russian sense of insecurity. Only one Chungus attack on the Japanese was recorded – an assault on one of the Japanese cavalry detachments that raided well behind the Russian lines in February 1905. The attack was of short duration; either because the bandits desisted on finding the detachment was not Russian, or because they encountered much stronger resistance, and less prospect of plunder, than a supply column would provide.

In Japanese-occupied areas Chinese authorities in general co-operated with the Japanese 'civil governors', who mostly confined their activities to sanitation, health and road maintenance, punished criminal acts by Japanese soldiers, and handed any Chinese offenders they caught over to the local police rather than punishing them themselves. The Russians, by contrast, exercised almost no control over their troops, destroyed rather than preserved, and inevitably blew up railway facilities and rail or road bridges as they withdrew. The Japanese quickly repaired these where possible, and though they did so for their own military purposes, their actions were naturally preferred by the Chinese locals to the Russian acts of destruction.

Witte woos the US public

Nicholas appointed Sergey Witte (actually 'Vitte'), a former Minister of Railways and later Finance Minister, to head Russia's delegation to the peace negotiations. In one sense it was an unusual choice, as Witte was unpopular with the court (which he despised), was hated by both tsar and tsaritsa, paid no respect to their religious beliefs or their anti-semitism, and had strongly opposed the policies that had brought on the war with Japan. He was considered vulgar, cynical, arrogant, boastful, and in present-day terms totally lacking in charisma. However, he was also by far the most able of the ministers Nicholas had inherited from his father; so in the current crisis Nicholas turned to him, and this proved to be one of his few good decisions.

Witte was aware that Japan had so far won the propaganda war, and set out to regain the initiative, starting on his passage across the Atlantic by cultivating the horde of European journalists travelling to report the negotiations. On arrival in the United States, he set out to woo the American press and public opinion, which on the whole favoured the Japanese David over the Russian Goliath, enlisting the advice of an old friend, E. J. Dillon, the St Petersburg correspondent of the London *Daily Telegraph*. Guided by Dillon he made favourable references to Japanese bravery and to Roosevelt's gifts as a leader, and treated all the Americans he met as equals. When he travelled by car or train, he always thanked and shook hands with the driver. Neither press nor public expected this type of behaviour from the representative of Europe's most autocratic regime, and it was therefore widely reported.

Of course all this was an act, as he admitted in his memoirs, and he did not bother to play it with Roosevelt, whom he

thought naïve, and who found him 'selfish and totally without ideals'; a vulgar contrast to the 'gentlemanly' Japanese. Witte probably felt no need to pose with Roosevelt, who could reasonably be assumed to be uneasy at the threat an expansionist Japan might in due course pose to the United States own recent acquisitions in the Pacific, Hawaii and the Philippines.

For press and public, the contrast between Witte's apparent openness and the uncommunicativeness of Foreign Minister Komura, who headed the Japanese delegation, began to swing opinion Russia's way. Nor, in Christian America, did Witte shrink from exploiting religion, demanding cancellation of the morning session of negotiations on Sunday 13 August, so that he and his delegation could attend church. Fearful of being branded as heathens, the Japanese decided their ambassador should also attend; but against a busload of Russians he stood no chance of making an impression; it was hardly coincidental that one of the hymns was sung to the tune of the Russian national anthem.

Witte also had some more tangible assets. The Japanese victories on land had been impressive, but not decisive. Russia had been beaten, but not conquered, and was still reinforcing her armies in Manchuria. Japan, on the other hand, would be hard put to maintain its forces even at their current level, and was heading towards bankruptcy. Its demands included payment of a large indemnity by Russia, and Witte succeeded in using this to depict the Japanese as avaricious money-grubbers, rather than the pure patriots previously lauded in the American press.

Apart from the indemnity, the Japanese demands included recognition of paramount Japanese rights in Korea, Russian evacuation

of Manchuria, provision of fishing rights for Japanese boats in Russia's Far Eastern coastal waters, retention of the Chinese Eastern Railway for commercial and industrial use only, cession to Japan of Port Arthur, Dalny, adjacent territory, most of the South Manchurian Railway, the whole of Sakhalin and all warships captured or interned in neutral ports.

The two main sticking-points were Sakhalin and the indemnity. Advised that Nicholas was prepared to continue the war

Portsmouth (left to right): Witte, Ambassador Rosen, President Theodore Roosevelt, Komura and Ambassador Kogoro.

rather than yield on either point, that four more Russian divisions had arrived in Manchuria, and that the Russian delegation was packing its bags, the Japanese cabinet met the Emperor on 28 August. That evening it telegraphed instructions to Komura to drop the demand for an indemnity, and also Sakhalin if necessary to reach agreement.

However, on information from the British that Nicholas would settle for retaining northern Sakhalin, the Japanese demand was modified to partition at the 50th parallel of latitude. At the final session, on 29 August, Komura tried to extract a payment of 1.2 million Yen for allowing Russia to retain northern Sakhalin, but when Witte refused, he dropped the demand. The Treaty of Portsmouth was signed on 5 September 1905, and came into effect on 16 October.

The Japanese public, unaware of the strategic and financial realities, reacted with fury at the lack of an indemnity and acquisition of only half of Sakhalin. Hundreds of police boxes in Tokyo were wrecked, over a thousand people killed or injured, and the offices of the *Kokumin*, the only newspaper to commend the treaty, were burned down. Martial law had to be introduced, and troops sent to guard the American Legation. A bizarre postscript to the disturbances was that on 11 September the *Mikasa* blew up and sank at its mooring in Sasebo with the loss of 251 lives, more than twice as many as the entire fleet lost at Tsushima. Romantics saw it as a samurai-style suicide in protest at the peace settlement, but the real cause was more mundane, carelessness of drunken sailors in the magazine.

Russian unrest overshadows defeat

In the vastness of Russia, defeat in what would now be termed a 'limited' or 'local' war, conducted almost entirely outside the country, and involving only the cession of half of a remote island, used mostly as a penal settlement, attracted little attention among a civilian population already lacking confidence in the regime. The defeats and subsequent revelations of incompetence merely intensified that lack of confidence in a country already preoccupied with revolutionary unrest, some of it financed by Colonel Akashi, but most of it engendered by the regime's own shortcomings.

Conscription of young male peasants and requisitioning of horses, both essential to an almost totally non-mechanised agriculture already suffering the effects of several successive poor harvests, created unrest in rural areas, and the diversion of much of the still relatively small industrial sector into war production depressed the economy somewhat. Among the intelligentsia, some took refuge in patriotism, others welcomed defeat as bringing the collapse of the autocracy closer.

Nicholas's response was to create Witte a count for his success in the peace negotiations, then use him to draft constitutional reforms, which created a parliament, the *Duma*, but gave it no real powers, and to embark on reforms of the armed forces. The First World War and revolutions of 1917 would show both sets of reforms to have been totally inadequate.

Inspiration and domination in the East

Despite Witte's success in the peace negotiations, Japan's victories on land and sea abruptly elevated it to the ranks of the Great Powers. As the first victory in modern times of an Asian over a European power, the war's outcome invigorated anti-imperialists such as Gandhi and Nehru in India and others in French Indo-China, Persia and Burma. In the shorter term, it inspired other modernising nationalists such as Sun Yat-sen, who toppled the old regime in China in 1911. Gradually, however, it dawned on Asian anti-imperialists that Japan's aim was not to liquidate imperialism but to impose its own.

In Japan the honours went to the army, reflecting its greater political influence, for battles that had been victorious but not decisive, rather than to the navy for its much more decisive wins. Several generals were promoted, a few to the highest rank of marshal, whereas Togo had to wait until just before his death in 1934 to be promoted to Admiral of the Fleet. The successful outcome of the war entrenched militarist expansionism, prompting the army eventually to usurp the dominant role in politics, and three junior officers who took part eventually became prime ministers – Generals Hirota and Tojo, both hanged for war crimes in 1946; and Admiral Suzuki, who headed the government that surrendered in 1945. Another junior officer, Lieutenant Isoroku Yamamoto, was in command of the Combined Fleet in 1941, the post Togo had held. Influenced by the successful British carrier-borne aircraft attack on the Italian Fleet at Taranto in November 1940, he sent a carrier task force against the American Pacific Fleet at Pearl Harbor.

In Russia, too, the army received more honour than the navy. Kuropatkin remained in office, commanded an army in the First World War, and was appointed Governor of Central Asia a few months before the regime collapsed in 1917. Admirals Rozhestvensky and Nebogatov and Captain Clapier de Colongue were court-martialled for surrendering the fleet, and General Stessel for surrendering Port Arthur. Rozhestvensky was acquitted; the others were sentenced to death, but Nicholas commuted their sentences to long terms of imprisonment.

In 1907 and 1910 Russo-Japanese agreements produced something resembling the 'division of spoils' Ito had vainly sought as an alternative to war in 1901. Japan recognised paramount Russian influence in Mongolia and northern Manchuria, while Russia acknowledged Japanese paramount influence in Korea and southern Manchuria.

One factor which helped maintain the West's generally pro-Japan stance was Japanese conduct towards prisoners of war and enemy wounded. At Mukden the Russians had to abandon five field hospitals full of patients too ill to be moved. A British observer (a Medical Corps lieutenant-colonel) with the Japanese noted that the hospitals contained about 600 Russians and 260 Japanese, and that the Russian medical staff had stayed with them. He reported that the provisions of the Geneva Convention:

were most rigidly carried out both in the letter and in the spirit by Japanese and Russians alike. The Japanese wounded found in them were receiving the greatest care and attention from the medical staff and nursing sisters. The Japanese, on their side, interfered in no way with the work of the hospitals so long as the Russian staff remained in them, and gave them every facility for carrying on their work. On the 26th March … all who wished were delivered over at the outposts under Article III of the convention

Japanese treatment of prisoners of war was also humane enough for many returned prisoners to compare it favourably with the way their own officers treated them. Clearly, Japanese brutality towards wounded and prisoners in the Second World War, or Soviet retention of German and Japanese prisoners of war as forced labour for up to 10 years after 1945 were products of the century rather than of the culture of Japanese or Russians. Since Japan escaped the carnage of the Western Front in the First World War, the image of war promoted by the militarists was of the easy victories of the Sino-Japanese War of 1894/95, and a version of the Russo-Japanese War sanitised to depict the peace as a gift from triumphant Japan to suppliant Russia.

Japan's expansionism continued, first with the annexation of Korea in 1910. Its modest contribution to the allied effort in the First World War was rewarded by League of Nations mandates over former German islands in the Pacific, and pressure was then put upon China. Starting with a set of 21 demands in 1915, it escalated to invasion of Manchuria in 1931, and the latter's detachment from China as the puppet state of Manchukuo in 1932, invasion of heartland China in 1937, of Soviet Far East frontier areas in 1938, and of Outer Mongolia in 1939. The Red Army's performance in those two years, especially in Mongolia, showed the Japanese military that the easy victories achieved over its tsarist predecessor were no longer possible.

This realisation was a major factor in the decision to attack south against French,

British, Dutch and American dependencies in December 1941, rather than north to aid Japan's German ally, then almost in the outskirts of Moscow, by opening a second front in the Soviet Far East. Stalin learned of this from a Soviet agent in Japan, Richard Sorge, and forthwith transferred a number of Siberian divisions to the west, where they helped greatly to win the battle of Moscow, Germany's first major land defeat of the war.

In August 1945 the Soviet Union joined the war against Japan, two days after the dropping of the first atomic bomb, and 12 hours before the second. For less than two weeks of fighting Stalin regained all that had been lost in 1905, and in addition seized the Kuriles Islands chain. In his victory speech on 2 September 1945 he said: 'The men of my generation have waited 40 years for this day ....'

The modernising of war

Among the most immediate and significant consequences of the war was its effect on military thinking. Since the last 'big' war, the Franco-Prussian War of 1870/71, technology had advanced greatly on land, and particularly at sea. Communication by telegraph had been available for decades, but radio was new, and though primitive it gave navies the same instant communication the telegraph had long provided for armies.

Navies were more affected than armies in other respects also, because there had been no major war at sea since the American Civil War of 1861–65. In that war, ships made of metal were in their infancy, as were breech-loading guns and turrets for them, steam propulsion was still seen largely as a supplement to sail, and the self-propelled 'Whitehead' torpedo had not yet been invented. The battles at sea in 1904/45 were the first between fleets made up entirely of metal warships, armoured and propelled wholly by steam. They were equipped with radio, breech-loading quick-firing guns, electric lighting, searchlights, and electric or hydraulic motors that enabled guns to be

turned or elevated mechanically. This allowed much larger and heavier guns to be installed, and their crews were protected within heavy armoured turrets. The only weapons systems added for later warfare were the aircraft (which first flew only in 1903), tank and submarine – both sides had some submarines, but neither used them. In most respects the warships of 1904/05 resembled those of the two world wars more than anything that preceded them.

The armies of both sides in the Franco-Prussian War had breech-loading rifles and artillery. The French also had a primitive machine-gun, but it was available only in small numbers and was so new and secret that no doctrine for its use had been developed, so it had little effect. Since then its use had become widespread in colonial wars, but the Russo-Japanese War was the first to involve battles between very large forces equipped entirely with breech-loading weapons, quick-firing guns and machine-guns. The tank had not yet been invented, and the only mechanical transport widely available was railways. However, the high rates of fire the new weapons could maintain placed a premium on entrenching, taking cover, camouflage and dispersal. Though perhaps less than in navies, there was still much for observers on land to learn.

The subjective eye

The war attracted a large number of professional observers. British, German, French, American, Austro-Hungarian and Italian officers were sent to the armies and navies of both sides; the British alone had 29 observers, including three lieutenant-generals, with the Japanese, and five with the Russians. The war over, they wrote their reports, but many drew sufficiently misleading or erroneous conclusions that they cast doubt on the wisdom of sending fighting men to act as analysts; indeed, some so totally lacked objectivity as to suggest their compilers had 'gone native'. For example, Captain (later Admiral) Pakenham, who spent most of the war with Togo's fleet, not merely defended but praised Togo's action in telling Tokyo the Port Arthur harbour entrance was blocked, when he knew it was not, and overall his reporting tended to depict Russia as his enemy, not just Japan's. Lieutenant-General Hamilton attributed the Japanese victory at Liaoyang to the triumph of 'the souls of the Japanese troops' over the inferior 'spiritual qualities' of the Russians, and a German account attributed it to a 'will to conquer'. An American naval officer with the 2nd Pacific Squadron described the Russian naval mentality as 'sluggish and underdeveloped', and the Japanese as 'trained and patriotic'. Kuropatkin conveniently excused his failures in similar terms: 'Our moral strength was less than that of the Japanese, and it was this inferiority rather than mistakes in generalship that caused our defeats.'

The reports overwhelmingly exalted the Japanese offensive spirit over Russian defensiveness. Certainly the results on land and water could be cited in support, but the conceptual leap that followed was less defensible. Apparently left out of consideration were: whether the defence had been badly conducted; the long time and enormous casualties General Nogi had incurred in overcoming the defences at Port Arthur; whether without skilful use of cover, such as uncut millet fields, and of camouflage and deception, the Japanese casualties would have been even higher; that Japan's losses in the war far exceeded Russia's; that Russia was beaten, but not conquered, and its Manchurian Army was stronger after Mukden than before it; in short, that the war had not been fought to a conclusion. The conceptual leap was that all the general staffs concluded that the defensive *per se* was always inferior to the defensive, and should be avoided. A French summary concluded to the contrary, but in 1914 the French Army, like all the others, went into battle committed to the *offensive a l'outrance*, and, like all the others, found barbed wire, trenches, machine-guns and quick-firing artillery minimised the gains and maximised the casualties.

Lessons 'learned' from the Russo-Japanese war had to be quickly unlearned. The Port Arthur experience, of large casualties for small gains against determined, well–armed and entrenched defenders, was seen as the exception, and the mobile warfare of northern Manchuria as the rule, but the First World War, at least on the (principal) Western Front, would show Port Arthur to be the rule, and mobile warfare the exception. It would take the internal combustion engine and its offspring, the tank, truck and aircraft, to resurrect mobile warfare, and to prove the 'lessons' of the First World War as misleading for the Second World War as the 'lessons' of the Russo-Japanese War had been for the First World War.

One example of attachment to the offensive was the Russian response to the use of their cavalry. The Cossacks had proved almost useless, and the Japanese cavalry saw little action. Instead of concluding that modern weapons and battlefield obstacles left very little prospect for cavalry, the Russians decided that better discipline (for the Japanese, better horsemanship) was all that was needed. Most foreign observers reached similar conclusions, and in 1914 all the armies had more cavalry than they could use, including the British, despite General Hamilton's caveat that new weapons generally reduced the horse to a means of transporting its rider more quickly to the places where he would fight on foot.

Japanese successes in outflanking the Russians created something of a fetish for outflanking movements. These were most attainable where forces were thinly spread, so that the ratio of force to space was small, as was the case in the Russo-Japanese War, and largely true of the Eastern Front in the First World War. But on the Western Front, the concentration of large, heavily–armed and entrenched forces in a relatively small space made the Japanese combination of frontal and outflanking attacks virtually inapplicable. The only solution strategists could find was to try by frontal assaults to create gaps through which the cavalry could pour to outflank, and hundreds of thousands of French and British infantrymen were slaughtered in attempts to create them.

Naval staffs similarly interpreted Tsushima as making victory dependent on clashes between fleets of battleships, but in reality winning the war at sea proved to depend in both world wars less on actions between battle fleets and more on large numbers of small ships, and in the Second World War also on smaller numbers of larger ships carrying aircraft, defending maritime supply lines against submarines, and to a lesser extent mines, convoying invading forces, putting them ashore and keeping them supplied. As submarines were not used in the Russo-Japanese War, and aircraft carriers did not exist, their potential remained undisclosed. However, torpedoes were used successfully by Togo's smaller ships, and mines sank two of his battleships within a few hours, while Russia had one sunk and another damaged in even less time. Yet no major navy had by 1914 developed adequate plans, let alone procured ships and

weaponry, to exploit or counter the threat from torpedo or mine.

Perhaps it is inevitable that military professionals in any country by nature prefer the offensive, and tend to reject evidence that suggests it is not always the better course. As late as the Second World War, training of both the German and the Soviet armies neglected the defensive, to the detriment of the Red Army in June to November 1941, and of the Wehrmacht in December. In other countries that initially misread the evidence, war was thought too serious to leave to generals; but Japan ultimately came to be run by its generals. If third-party military observers could be mesmerised by Japan's successes, it is not surprising that the Japanese military were mesmerised most of all. Their biggest gamble, the decision in 1941 to attack the United States, rested in stubbornly held belief in the superiority of the 'spiritual' over the material. That belief received its initial impetus in the Russo-Japanese War.

Further reading

Warner, Denis & Peggy, *The Tide at Sunrise; a History of the Russo-Japanese War,* Angus and Robertson (London, 1975)

Westwood, J.N., *Japan against Russia, 1904–5: a new look at the Russo-Japanese War,* New York State University Press (1986)

Schimmelpenninck van der Oye, David, *Towards the Rising Sun: Russian Ideologies of Empire and the Path to War,* Northern Illinois University Press (2001)

The Russo-Japanese War: Reports from Officers Attached to the Japanese Forces in the Field, reprinted with introduction by Sebastian Dobson, 5 Vols; London, Ganesha, Tokyo, Edition Synapse (2000)

Von Donat, Karl (trans.), *The Russo-Japanese War. Reports prepared in the Historical Section of the German General Staff,* Hugh Rees (London 1909, Vol. I; 1913, Vol. 2), reprinted Ch'eng Wen (Taipei, 1971)

Nish, I., *The origins of the Russo-Japanese war,* London, Longman, (1985)

Corbett, J. S., *Maritime operations in the Russo-Japanese war,* Navval Institute Press, (1995)

Walder, D., *The short victorious war: The Russo-Japanese conflict 1904–05,* London, Harper Collins, (1974)

Index

Figures in **bold** refer to illustrations

Related titles from Osprey Publishing

ELITE (ELI)

**Uniforms, equipment, tactics and personalities
of troops and commanders**

MEN-AT-ARMS (MAA)

**Uniforms, equipment, history
and organisation of troops**

CAMPAIGN (CAM)

**Strategies, tactics and battle experiences
of opposing armies**

ESSENTIAL HISTORIES (ESS)

**Concise overviews of major wars
and theatres of war**

NEW VANGUARD (NVG)

**Design, development and operation
of the machinery of war**

WARRIOR (WAR)

**Motivation, training, combat experiences
and equipment of individual soldiers**

ORDER OF BATTLE (OOB)

**Unit-by-unit troop movements and
command strategies of major battles**
Contact us for more details – see below

AIRCRAFT OF THE ACES (ACES)

**Experiences and achievements
of 'ace' fighter pilots**

AVIATION ELITE (AEU)

Combat histories of fighter or bomber units
Contact us for more details – see below

COMBAT AIRCRAFT (COM)

**History, technology and crews
of military aircraft**
Contact us for more details – see below

To order any of these titles, or for more information on Osprey Publishing, contact:
Osprey Direct (UK) Tel: +44 (0)1933 443863 Fax: +44 (0)1933 443849 E-mail: info@ospreydirect.co.uk
Osprey Direct (USA) c/o MBI Publishing Toll-free: 1 800 826 6600 Phone: 1 715 294 3345
Fax: 1 715 294 4448 E-mail: info@ospreydirectusa.com
www.ospreypublishing.com

FIND OUT MORE ABOUT OSPREY

❏ Please send me a FREE trial issue of Osprey Military Journal

❏ Please send me the latest listing of Osprey's publications

❏ I would like to subscribe to Osprey's e-mail newsletter

Title/rank _____

Name _____

Address _____

_____

_____

_____

Postcode/zip _____

State/country _____

E-mail _____

Which book did this card come from?

_____

❏ I am interested in military history

My preferred period of military history is _____

❏ I am interested in military aviation

My preferred period of military aviation is _____

I am interested in *(please tick all that apply)*

❏ general history   ❏ militaria   ❏ model making

❏ wargaming   ❏ re-enactment

Please send to:

USA & Canada:
Osprey Direct USA, c/o MBI Publishing,
PO Box 1, 729 Prospect Ave, Osceola, WI 54020, USA

UK, Europe and rest of world:
Osprey Direct UK, PO Box 140, Wellingborough,
Northants, NN8 2FA, United Kingdom

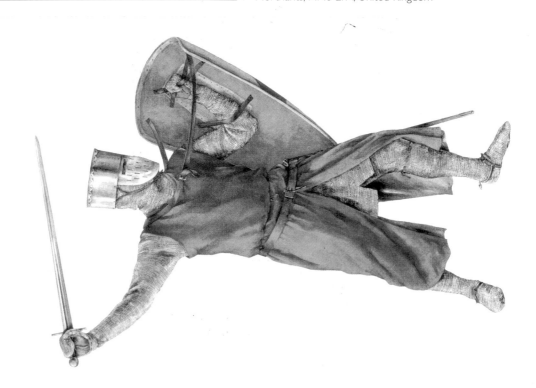

OSPREY
PUBLISHING

www.ospreypublishing.com

call our telephone hotline
for a free information pack

USA & Canada: 1-800-826-6600
UK, Europe and rest of world call:
+44 (0) 1933 443 863

Young Guardsman
Figure taken from *Warrior 22:
Imperial Guardsman 1799–1815*
Published by Osprey
Illustrated by Christa Hook

Knight, c.1190
Figure taken from *Warrior 1: Norman Knight 950 – 1204AD*
Published by Osprey
Illustrated by Christa Hook

POSTCARD